ECONOMIC ISSUES, PROBLEMS AND PERSPECTIVES

FEDERAL DEFICITS AND DEBT

IMPACTS AND ISSUES

ECONOMIC ISSUES, PROBLEMS AND PERSPECTIVES

Additional books in this series can be found on Nova's website under the Series tab.

Additional e-books in this series can be found on Nova's website under the eBooks tab.

ECONOMIC ISSUES, PROBLEMS AND PERSPECTIVES

FEDERAL DEFICITS AND DEBT

IMPACTS AND ISSUES

JAMIE MALONE
EDITOR

New York

Library of Congress Cataloging-in-Publication Data

ISBN: 978-1-53610-268-0

Published by Nova Science Publishers, Inc. † New York

CONTENTS

PREFACE

The federal government incurs a budget deficit (also known as a net deficit) when its total outgoing payments (outlays) exceed the total money it collects (revenues). If instead federal revenues are greater than outlays, then the federal government generates a surplus. Deficits are measured over the course of a defined period of time—in the case of the federal government, a fiscal year. Over time, persistent budget deficits can hamper economic growth. Federal debt, either publicly held or intragovernmental, is funded through private capital. In the absence of federal debt, a portion of such funding would likely have been used on private investment projects that could increase the future productive capabilities of the economy. Large or rapidly increasing debt levels could also make the economy more susceptible to a recession, although that dynamic has not manifested itself in the United States. This book explores distinctions in the concept and composition of deficits and debt, explains how these two measures interact, and discusses their possible effects on the economy. Furthermore, the book discusses the size of projected budget deficits; how much the deficit would need to be reduced to return to long-term sustainability; analyzes alternative time frames for reducing the deficit; and discusses broad policy choices for reducing the deficit.

In: Federal Deficits and Debt
Editor: Jamie Malone

ISBN: 978-1-53610-268-0

Chapter 1

DEFICITS AND DEBT: ECONOMIC EFFECTS AND OTHER ISSUES*

Grant A. Driessen

SUMMARY

The federal government incurs a budget deficit (also known as a net deficit) when its total outgoing payments (outlays) exceed the total money it collects (revenues). If instead federal revenues are greater than outlays, then the federal government generates a surplus. Deficits are measured over the course of a defined period of time—in the case of the federal government, a fiscal year.

Debt measurements may be taken at any point in time and represent the accumulation of all previous government borrowing activity, from private citizens, institutions, foreign governments, and other parts of the federal government. Federal debt increases when there are net budget deficits and outflows made for federal credit programs, which combine to represent debt held by the public. Federal debt also rises through increases in intragovernmental debt, which is generated by trust fund surpluses that are used to finance other government activity.

Federal budgeting practices create a system where deficits and debt are interdependent: budget deficits increase federal debt levels, which in turn increase future net deficits. The nature of the relationship between

* This is an edited, reformatted and augmented version of a Congressional Research Service publication, R44383, dated February 17, 2016.

deficits and debt varies depending on the type of debt considered. Budget deficits are the principal contributor to debt held by the public.

The contribution of deficits to intragovernmental debt is less certain than their contribution to debt held by the public. All else equal, increases in net trust fund deficits will lead to increases in total budget deficits but decreases in intragovernmental debt.

The interest payments made on publicly held debt instruments contribute directly to federal deficits. Holders of federal debt are compensated by receiving interest payments from Treasury. Intragovernmental debt does not contribute to future deficits.

The combination of persistent budget deficits and a large and increasing federal debt has generated discussions over the long-term sustainability of current budget projections. Federal budget deficits have declined from 9.8% of gross domestic product (GDP) in FY2009 to 2.5% of GDP in FY2015. However, recent estimates forecast that the government will run deficits in every year through FY2026. Federal debt totaled $18.922 trillion at the end of calendar year 2015, and as a percentage of GDP is at its highest value since the end of World War II; $13.673 trillion of that debt was held by the public.

Over time, persistent budget deficits can hamper economic growth. Federal debt, either publicly held or intragovernmental, is funded through private capital. In the absence of federal debt, a portion of such funding would likely have been used on private investment projects that could increase the future productive capabilities of the economy. Large or rapidly increasing debt levels could also make the economy more susceptible to a recession, although that dynamic has not manifested itself in the United States.

INTRODUCTION

The combination of persistent budget deficits and a large and increasing federal debt has generated discussions over the long-term sustainability of current budget projections. Federal budget deficits have declined from 9.8% of gross domestic product (GDP) in FY2009 to 2.5% of GDP in FY2015. However, recent estimates forecast that the government will run deficits (i.e., federal expenditures will exceed revenues) in every year through FY2026. Federal debt totaled $18.922 trillion at the end of calendar year 2015, and as a percentage of GDP is at its highest value since the end of World War II; $13.673 trillion of that debt was held by the public.

This report explores distinctions in the concept and composition of deficits and debt, explains how these two measures interact, and discusses their possible effects on the economy.

BACKGROUND

What Is a Deficit?

The federal government incurs a deficit (also known as a net deficit) when its total outgoing payments (outlays) exceed the total money it collects (revenues). If instead federal revenues are greater than outlays, then the federal government generates a surplus. A balanced budget describes the case where federal receipts equal federal expenditures.[1] The size of a deficit or surplus is equal to the difference between the levels of spending and receipts. Deficits are measured over the course of a defined period of time—in the case of the federal government, a fiscal year.[2]

Federal budget outcomes incorporate both "on-budget" activities, which represent the majority of federal taxes and spending, and "off-budget" government activities, which include revenues and outlays from Social Security trust funds and the Postal Service. For federal credit programs, the subsidy cost of government activities is included in deficit and surplus calculations.[3]

Net deficit levels are dependent upon both economic and legislative conditions. More robust economic periods have generally produced lower net deficits (or higher net surpluses), due to increases in receipts (from greater tax revenues) and reduced expenditures (from decreased demand for public assistance). From FY1962 to FY2015, the average net deficit equaled 2.6% of annual GDP. In FY2015, that amount had a dollar value of just over $460 billion.[4] In the FY1962-FY2015 period, the government generated a surplus on five occasions: in FY1969, and from FY1998 through FY2001. In every other year of the period, the federal government incurred a net deficit.[5]

What Is the Debt?

The federal debt level represents the total amount of money that the government owes to its creditors, which include private citizens, institutions, foreign governments, and other parts of the federal government. Debt measurements may be taken at any point in time and represent the accumulation of all previous government borrowing activity. Federal debt increases when there are net budget deficits, outflows made for federal credit programs (net of the subsidy costs already included in deficit calculations), and increases in intragovernmental borrowing.

Federal debt calculations also include the cost of federal credit programs.[6] Federal credit programs include loans issued for college tuition payments, small business programs, and other activities the government may seek to support. In those cases, debt levels increase as additional loans are granted, and decrease as money for such programs is repaid.

Intragovernmental debt is generated when trust funds, revolving funds, and special funds receive money from tax payments, fees, or other revenue sources that is not immediately needed to make payments. In those cases, the surpluses are used to finance other government activities, and Government Account Series (GAS) securities are issued to the trust fund. GAS securities may then be redeemed when trust fund expenditures exceed revenue levels. *Intragovernmental debt may be thought of as money that one part of the government owes another part.*

The Department of the Treasury is responsible for managing federal debt. The primary objective of Treasury's debt management strategy is to fulfill the government's borrowing needs at the lowest cost over time.[7] Treasury finances federal borrowing activities by issuing government-backed securities that generate interest payments for their owners. Treasury securities are typically sold to the public through an auction process, and have maturity periods (the length of time which they are held before repayment) of anywhere from several weeks to 30 years.[8]

Comparing Debt Held by the Public and Intragovernmental Debt

Federal debt may be divided into two major categories: (1) debt held by the public, which is the sum of accrued net deficits and outstanding money from federal credit programs; and (2) intragovernmental debt. As of December 31, 2015, the amount of federal debt outstanding was $18.922 trillion, with 72.3% of that debt held by the public and 27.7% held as intragovernmental debt.[9] *Table 1* summarizes the characteristics of debt held by the public and intragovernmental debt.

Table 1. Features of Debt Held by the Public and Intragovernmental Debt

	Publicly Held Debt	Intragovernmental Debt
Origin	Budget deficits and the federal loan portfolio	Federal trust fund surpluses
Ownership	Individuals and institutions (domestic and foreign); state and local governments; foreign governments	Federal government accounts
Debt outstanding	$13.673 trillion (72.3%)	$5.250 trillion (27.7%)
Share of marketable securities	$13.183 trillion (99.8%)	$0.024 trillion (0.2%)
Financial market presence	Debt issuances may compete for private assets exchanged in the financial market	Debt issuances do not appear in public markets and thus do not compete for private assets

Source: U.S. Treasury, Monthly Statement of the Public Debt, December 2015: available at http://treasurydirect.gov/govt/reports/pd/mspd/2015/opds122015.pdf.
Notes: Debt values as of December 31, 2015.

Individuals, firms, the Federal Reserve, state and local governments, and foreign governments are eligible to purchase publicly held debt. Such debt may be acquired directly through the auction process from which most publicly held debt is initially sold or on the secondary market if the debt is deemed "marketable", or eligible for resale.[10] The total amount of publicly held debt outstanding was $13.673 trillion as of December 31, 2015. The majority of publicly held debt is marketable, and includes all Treasury Notes, Bonds, Bills, Treasury Inflation Protected Securities (TIPS), and Floating Rate Notes (FRNs) issued by Treasury. Non-marketable debt held by the public is comprised of U.S. Savings Bonds, State and Local Government Securities (SLGS), and other, smaller issues. As of December 31, 2015, 96.4% of publicly held issues, or $13.183 trillion, was marketable.

Intragovernmental debt is held by components of the federal government. Intragovernmental debt issuances are almost exclusively nonmarketable, as marketable debt comprised only $0.024 trillion (0.5%) of the $5.250 trillion in total intragovernmental debt on December 31, 2015. The majority of nonmarketable intragovernmental debt was held by trust funds devoted to Social Security and military and federal worker retirement. Marketable intragovernmental debt is composed primarily of debt held by the Federal Financing Bank, which is a government corporation created to reduce the cost of federal borrowing.

Since intragovernmental debt is held only in government accounts, such debt cannot be accessed by the institutions outside the federal government. Conversely, the bonds that finance publicly held debt activity may compete for assets in private and financial markets. Public debt issues may be a particularly attractive collateral option on the secondary market if the federal government is perceived as a safe credit risk.

DEFICIT AND DEBT INTERACTION

Federal budgeting practices create a system where deficits and debt are interdependent; budget deficits increase federal debt levels, which in turn increase future net deficits because of the need to service higher interest payments on the nation's debt. The nature of the relationship between deficits and debt varies depending on the type of debt considered. This section describes the relationship between federal deficits and debt.

How Deficits Contribute to Debt

Budget deficits are the principal contributor to debt held by the public. In order to finance budget deficits, Treasury sells debt instruments. The value of those debt holdings (which include interest payments) represents the vast majority of publicly held debt. From FY1962 to FY2015, annual nominal budget deficits of the federal government summed to $11.772 trillion: over the same period, total debt held by the public increased by $12.869 trillion.[11]

The contribution of deficits to intragovernmental debt is less certain than their contribution to debt held by the public. When trust funds run deficits, they require redemptions of intragovernmental debt to remain solvent; this causes total intragovernmental debt to decline. All else equal, when intragovernmental debt declines Treasury increases publicly held debt issuances in order to finance government operations. This scenario changes the composition of federal debt, but the total debt level is held constant. Changes in trust fund financing are one of many potential causes for changes in budget outcomes. The budgetary conditions of trust funds are not necessarily reflective of the budgetary situation of the entire federal government.

Figure 1 shows the relative effect of deficits and other activities on changes in federal debt levels from FY1962 through FY2015. Over that time period, annual contributions of federal deficits to changes in nominal debt have been twice as large (2.6% of GDP) as other contributions to debt (1.3% of GDP). Deficit levels increased over this time period, as the average deficit from FY1989 through FY2015 (3.0% of GDP) was higher than from FY1962 through FY1988 (2.3% of GDP). However, the share of deficit contributions to changes in nominal debt has declined in recent years, as expansions in the federal loan portfolio and in intragovernmental debt have increased the average contribution of other debt-generating activities from 0.7% of GDP from FY1962 through FY1988 to 1.9% of GDP from FY1989 through FY2015.

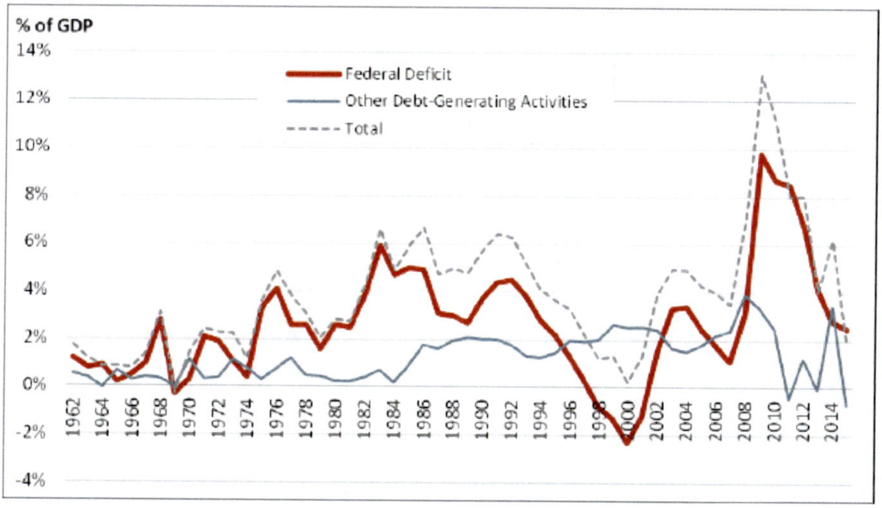

Source: Office of Management and Budget, Historical Tables 1.2 and 7.1. CRS calculations.

Notes: "Total" represents the dollar increase or decrease in debt levels over the course of the year, measured as a percentage of GDP. This notion differs from the change in real federal debt (also measured as a percentage of GDP), which is affected by inflationary forces.

Figure 1. Contribution of Deficits to Debt, FY1962-FY2015. (As a % of GDP)

How Debt Contributes to Deficits

Publicly held debt contributes directly to federal deficits through interest payments on debt issuances. Interest payments are made to both debt held by the public and intragovernmental debt. As the government serves as buyer and seller of intragovernmental debt, interest payments on those holdings do not affect the federal budget deficit.[12] However, interest payments made on publicly held debt represent new federal spending, and are recorded in the budget as outlays when payments are made. *Interest represents the cost that the government incurs when it opts to finance spending through borrowing rather than through increased revenues. In budgetary terms, net interest payments represent the total amount of money paid from the government to debt holders in a given time period.*[13]

For investors, the purchase of a debt issuance represents both a loss of liquidity relative to currency holdings (money paid for the debt holding can be used immediately, while the debt issuance may only be resold on the secondary market or held until the date of maturity) and an opportunity cost (the money used for the purchase could have been spent on other items, invested elsewhere, or saved). Debt holders are compensated for those costs by receiving interest payments from Treasury on their issuances.

Determinants of Net Interest Payments

The amount of net interest payments owed by the federal government depends on the existing stock, or total, of federal debt and the interest rate on outstanding debt instruments. The structure of the interest payments may be fixed or variable, depending on the type of debt holding. In either case, the terms of interest are agreed to in advance of sale. Interest rates on debt vehicles are largely determined by prevailing economic conditions. Situations where the private cost of borrowing (interest rate) is high will raise interest rates on federal debt and thereby increase net interest payments. Increases in the amount of existing debt will also lead to a rise in net interest payments, as it increases the base on which a given interest rate is applied.

From FY1962 to FY2015, net interest payments averaged 1.9% of annual GDP, a figure equivalent to about $340 billion in 2015 dollars. High interest rates and increasing debt levels caused the net interest burden to peak in the 1980s and 1990s. Recent net interest payments have been lower than their long-term averages; in FY2015, net interest payments were $223 billion, or 1.3% of annual GDP. Those low payments are the product of historically low interest rates, as real debt levels are at their highest value since the end of World War II. Unless the federal debt is significantly reduced, net interest payments will likely increase significantly if interest rates shift toward their long-term averages. In its most recent forecast, CBO projects that real net interest payments will rise to 3.0% of GDP by FY2026.[14]

The level of net interest payments generated by debt holdings can have a significant effect on the federal deficit. One way to measure this effect is through the primary deficit, which is equal to the net budget deficit excluding the effect of net interest payments. The primary deficit averaged 0.7% of GDP from FY1962 to FY2015, a far smaller figure than the 2.6% of GDP average recorded by the budget deficit over the same time period. While the federal government only recorded a budget surplus five times from FY1962 to FY2014, in 16 other years it registered a primary surplus, most recently in 2007.

ECONOMIC EFFECTS OF DEFICITS AND DEBT

Historical Trends

The historical trends of federal deficit and debt levels are displayed in *Table 2*. Along with averages of the real burden of deficits, debt stock, and real GDP growth, there is also a measurement of average growth in nominal GDP, which captures total economic output without adjusting for inflation. All else equal, higher levels of nominal GDP make a given amount of debt easier to repay by eroding its real value. For example, the highest measurement of debt since 1940 occurred in 1946, when the federal debt level was 118.9% of GDP, or $271 billion in nominal FY1946 dollars. In contrast, $271 billion was equivalent to only 1.5% of GDP in FY2015.[15] Increases in nominal GDP may be caused by productivity increases, economic inflation—which measures the purchasing power of currency—or a combination of each factor.[16]

Of the federal activity shown in *Table 2*, the highest annual deficits were accrued from FY1941 to FY1955, largely due to financing U.S. involvement in World War II. However, nominal economic growth was also relatively high during that time period, which slowed the rise in the stock of debt. From FY1956 to FY1970, average annual growth in nominal GDP slowed to 6.5%, but deficits were roughly one-tenth of those in the previous 15 years, causing average debt to decline over the course of the period. FY1971-FY1985 experienced increases in both deficits and nominal economic growth (driven largely by inflationary forces), holding the stock of debt relatively constant. From FY1984 to FY1999, average deficits were nearly identical to those in the previous 15 years, but nominal economic growth slowed, leading to a rise in the stock of debt as a percentage of GDP. That rise accelerated since FY2001, due to the combination of deficit increases and the decline in nominal economic growth. The debt burden decreased slightly from FY2014 (103.2% of GDP) to FY2015 (101.7% of GDP); before FY2014, the FY2015 debt burden had not been reached since FY1947.

Table 2. Trends in Deficits and Debt, FY1941-FY2015

Time Period	Average Annual Deficit (% of GDP)	Average Annual Growth, Real GDP (%)	Average Annual Growth, Nominal GDP (%)	Stock of Debt, End of Period (% of GDP)
FY1941-FY1955	6.3	5.3	9.9	67.4
FY1956-FY1970	0.6	3.7	6.5	36.3
FY1971-FY1985	3.0	3.2	9.2	42.6
FY1986-FY2000	2.2	3.4	6.0	55.5
FY2001-FY2015	3.9	1.8	4.0	101.7

Source: Office of Management and Budget, Historical Tables 1.2 and 7.1; Bureau of Economic Analysis, National Income and Product Accounts, Table 1.1.3. CRS calculations.

Notes: Unlike real GDP, nominal GDP is affected by inflationary forces, which increases average growth rates. "Stock of Debt, End of Period" represents the total debt recorded at the end of each time period (e.g., at the end of FY1955 for the FY1941-FY1955 time period).

Possible Explanations for Deficits

The government may choose to generate short-run budget deficits for a few reasons. Deficit financing, or payment for federal government activity at least partly through debt increases, increases the total level of spending in the economy. Most economists believe that the implementation of deficit financing can be used to generate a short-term stimulus effect, either for a particular industry or for the entire economy. In their view, increases in expenditures and tax reductions can be used to generate employment opportunities and consumer spending and reduce the intensity of stagnant economic periods. Deficit financing is a less effective countercyclical strategy when it leads to "crowding out." Crowding out occurs when government financing merely replaces private sector funding instead of inducing new economic activity.

Deficit financing may also be used as part of a structurally balanced budget strategy, which alters government tax and spending levels to smooth the effect of business cycles. Smoothing budgetary changes may reduce the economic shocks deficits induce among businesses and households.

Governments may also use federal deficits or surpluses to spread the payment burden of longterm projects across generations. This sort of intergenerational redistribution is one justification for the creation of long-run trust funds, such as those devoted to Social Security.

In the long run, the effect of budget deficit outcomes depends on economic conditions, the stock and composition of debt, and the policy goals under consideration.

Effects of Persistent Deficits

Although there are some cases where deficit financing may be advisable, long-run generation of deficits causes publicly held debt accumulation that is generally thought to inhibit economic growth. Deficit financing tends to crowd out greater levels of private investment in better economic conditions. Such debt eventually must be repaid, either through spending reductions, tax increases, or combination of the two, and may also generate crowding out that could reduce future economic productivity.

In extreme cases, large or rapidly increasing debt levels may also have unintended macroeconomic effects. If potential buyers of U.S. debt issuances lose confidence in the ability of the federal government to repay its debt, ensuing increases in the supply of money through debt financing (known as debt monetization) may lead to rising interest costs or price inflation. Such a scenario could harm economic output and increase the chances of a recession. Though it is difficult to predict when such a reduction in market confidence would take place, such an event would likely be related at least in part to the amount of real debt (measured as a percentage of GDP).[17] There are many instances where this phenomenon has occurred abroad, but no examples in modern U.S. history.

Deficit and Debt Outlook

The short-term deficit and debt outlook of the federal government has improved in recent years. The FY2015 real deficit was equal to 2.5% of GDP, and marked the sixth consecutive decline after hitting its post-war peak in FY2009. Moreover, reductions in intragovernmental debt and improved economic growth led to a real decline in total debt in FY2015 for the first time since FY2001. However, both deficits and debt are projected to increase in each year of the current budget window, which runs through FY2026. CBO, GAO, and the Administration agree that the current set of fiscal policies will lead to an unsustainable debt burden if left unchanged in the long run. In its latest economic forecast, the CBO projected that the total burden of U.S. debt held by the public would steadily increase over the course of the budget window, from 75.6% of GDP in FY2016 to 86.1% of GDP in FY2026.[18] Addressing the potential consequences of those projections will likely involve policy adjustments that reduce the occurrences and intensity of budget deficits, either through tax increases, further reductions in spending, or a combination of the two.

End Notes

[1] For a more thorough discussion of budget concepts, see Office of Management and Budget, FY 2017 Budget: Analytical Perspectives, February 2016.

[2] As compared to the calendar year, the federal fiscal year runs from October of the previous year through September of the current year. For example, FY2016 began on October 1, 2015, and will end on September 30, 2016.

[3] The Federal Credit Reform Act of 1992 (P.L. 101-58) defines subsidy costs as "the estimated long-term cost to the government of a loan guarantee, calculated on a net present value basis, excluding administrative costs." Subsidy costs therefore represent a projection of the final cost to the government of a credit program, and not the inflow or outflow of money for the activity. For more information about subsidy costs and their effect on the federal budget, see CRS Report R44193, Federal Credit Programs: Comparing Fair Value and the Federal Credit Reform Act (FCRA), by Raj Gnanarajah.

[4] Except where otherwise noted, all deficit and debt figures will be expressed as a percentage of GDP.

[5] Office of Management and Budget, Fiscal Year 2016 Historical Tables, Table 1.1, available at https://www.whitehouse.gov/sites/default/files/omb/budget/fy2016/assets/hist.pdf.

[6] For more information about the accounting methods used in deficit and debt calculations, see CRS Report R43811, Cash Versus Accrual Basis of Accounting: An Introduction, by Raj Gnanarajah, and CRS Report R44002, Cash Versus Accrual Accounting: Tax Policy Considerations, by Raj Gnanarajah and Mark P. Keightley.

[7] U.S. Department of the Treasury, Duties & Functions of the U.S. Department of the Treasury, available at http://www.treasury.ogv/about/role-of-treasury/.

[8] For more information about Treasury's debt management practices, see CRS Report R40767, How Treasury Issues Debt, by Grant A. Driessen.

[9] Unless otherwise noted, federal debt totals are taken from U.S. Treasury, Monthly Statement of the Public Debt, December 2015, available at http://treasurydirect.gov/govt/reports/pd/mspd//opds122015.pdf.

[10] The Banking Act of 1935 (P.L. 74-305) prohibited the Federal Reserve from purchasing Treasury securities directly (at auction). The Federal Reserve may purchase Treasury securities on the secondary market.

[11] Office of Management and Budget, Historical Tables 1.1 and 7.1, available at https://www.whitehouse.gov/omb/budget/Historicals.

[12] Although intragovernmental debt does not affect net interest payments, shifts in certain types of intragovernmental debt may serve as a signal of future budgetary challenges. A notable example of such signaling may be seen with the increases in intragovernmental debt held by trust funds devoted to Social Security. Intragovernmental debt from those funds began increasing in the 1980s, as the entry of the "Baby Boomer" generation into the workforce increased payments into the Social Security system, and produced surpluses in Social Security trust funds. However, all else equal, the eventual retirement of those same workers has led to payments from Social Security trust funds exceeding revenues, thereby drawing down from excess funds in those accounts.

[13] The combined interest paid on debt held by the public and intragovernmental debt is known as gross interest payments.

[14] Congressional Budget Office, The Budget and Economic Outlook: 2016 to 2026, January 2016.

[15] With positive economic growth, it is possible to simultaneously experience a year-over-year increase in nominal debt and decrease in real debt. The federal government experienced this most recently from FY2000 to FY2001, when nominal debt increased by $141 billion (from $5.629 trillion to $5.770 trillion), but real debt decreased by 0.9% of GDP (from 55.5% to 54.6%).

[16] Because real GDP measures adjust for the effects of inflation, average nominal GDP growth from FY1941-FY2015 (7.1%) exceeds measures of real GDP growth over the same period. As measured by the Bureau of Economic Analysis' National Income and Product Accounts (Table 1.1.3), real GDP grew by an annual average of 3.5% from FY1941 to FY2015.

[17] For more information on the economic effects of deficits and debt, see CRS Report R40770, The Sustainability of the Federal Budget Deficit: Market Confidence and Economic Effects, by Marc Labonte.

[18] Congressional Budget Office, The Budget and Economic Outlook: 2016 to 2026, January 2016.

In: Federal Deficits and Debt
Editor: Jamie Malone
ISBN: 978-1-53610-268-0

Chapter 2

REDUCING THE BUDGET DEFICIT: OVERVIEW OF POLICY ISSUES*

Marc Labonte

SUMMARY

The federal budget deficit was the largest it has been since World War II as a percentage of GDP from 2009 to 2012, peaking at 10.1% of GDP. This occurred because spending reached its highest share of GDP since 1945 and revenues reached their lowest share of GDP since 1950. Since then, the deficit has declined to a projected 2.8% of GDP in 2014, which is still above the 1946 to 2008 average. Over the next 25 years, deficits are projected to become very large again under current law.

The recent decline in the deficit is partly due to improvements in the economy, the expiration of temporary measures taken in response to the recession, and spending cuts (mainly to discretionary spending). Spending was cut by the Budget Control Act of 2011 (BCA; P.L. 112-25) and the reduction in overseas contingency operations (OCO), primarily in Iraq and Afghanistan. Since September 2008, legislative changes to spending have added a cumulative $1.12 trillion to deficits and legislative changes to revenues, mainly the extension of expiring tax provisions, have added $1.75 trillion to deficits, excluding resulting interest costs.

Looking forward, several uncertainties are inherent in the baseline that may lead to different outcomes than projected. There have been large errors

* This is an edited, reformatted and augmented version of a Congressional Research Service publication, R43680, dated August 7, 2014.

to budget projections historically, in part because economic forecasting is subject to large errors. The budget has also proven to be highly sensitive to recessions, and CBO does not project a recession in its 10-year projection. Budget projections also do not assume any significant changes in spending on future wars or disasters. The baseline projection follows current law, assuming that the "doc fix" and tax "extenders" will expire as scheduled. If Congress temporarily extends either, as it has done regularly in the past, the deficit will be larger than projected.

In the long run, legislative changes will be needed to reduce spending or increase taxes to keep the debt on a sustainable path. Postponing action requires larger changes to be made in the long run, and limits the ability to phase in changes gradually. Economists view the debt as currently unsustainable because it is projected to grow faster than gross domestic product (GDP) indefinitely under current policy, causing an ever growing share of national income to be devoted to servicing the debt. The main source of long-term fiscal unsustainability is the growth in elderly entitlement spending. In particular, spending on major health programs, such as Medicare and Medicaid, is assumed to continue to grow faster than GDP, as it has historically. Overall, mandatory spending has grown as a share of GDP, rising from 4.7% of GDP, when data were first compiled in 1962, to a projected 12.3% of GDP in 2014, and is projected to continue rising. By contrast, discretionary spending has fallen from 12.3% of GDP in 1962 to a projected 6.8% of GDP in 2014, and under the baseline it is projected to decline to its lowest share of GDP ever, primarily because of the BCA's statutory caps. Revenues are projected to stay near their historical average over the next 10 years.

Economic theory predicts that deficits have a stimulative effect on the economy during recessions, but harm economic growth by resulting in an increase in interest rates or the trade deficit during economic booms. Thus, the state of the economy is a consideration for the timing of deficit reduction.

Options for deficit reduction on the spending side are constrained by the fact that Social Security, Medicare, net interest, and defense discretionary spending make up almost two-thirds of total spending. On the revenue side, 80% of revenue is raised by income and payroll taxes.

INTRODUCTION

The federal budget has been in deficit (i.e., spending has exceeded revenues) since 2002, and deficits were significantly larger from 2009 to 2012 than in any other year since World War II. As a result, the federal debt held by the public increased from 39% of gross domestic product (GDP) in 2008 to 72% of GDP in 2013, which was its highest share of GDP since after World War II.[1]

From 1946 to 2008, budget deficits averaged 1.7% of GDP and exceeded 5% of GDP only three times (equaling 7.2% in 1946, 6.0% in 1983, and 5.1% of GDP in 1985). The budget deficit was 10.1% of GDP in 2009, falling to 7% of GDP in 2012.[2] The fiscal outlook has improved significantly since then, although the budget is projected to remain in deficit under current policy. In 2014, the baseline deficit is projected to be $492 billion or 2.8% of GDP. Not since the end of World War II has the deficit fallen so much, so quickly. Despite the improvement, the deficit still remains above its historical average.

In the past, persistent deficits have proven sustainable because periods of moderate growth in the debt relative to GDP have been followed by periods when debt fell relative to GDP (typically, because the debt grew more slowly than GDP). Current policy is unsustainable because projected deficits are large enough to cause the federal debt to continuously grow faster than national income. This increase is projected to be gradual—the debt does not increase relative to GDP until 2019, is five percentage points higher by 2024, and reaches 100% of GDP by 2036 or sooner. At some point, spending cuts or revenue increases will be needed to restore fiscal sustainability, although the recent decline in the deficit has provided policymakers more flexibility on the timing of these changes.

Congress has expressed interest in examining policy options to reduce the deficit. The Congressional Research Service (CRS) does not take a position on the best way to reduce the deficit. This report organizes and presents information to help policymakers frame the debate. This report first discusses the size of projected budget deficits, then discusses how much the deficit would need to be reduced to return to long-term sustainability, then analyzes alternative time frames for reducing the deficit, and finally discusses broad policy choices for reducing the deficit. This report assumes a familiarity with basic budget terms and concepts.

Why Did Deficits Rise and Then Decline?

The budget deficit increased by almost $1 trillion between 2008 and 2009. As shown in *Table 1*, this increase was not anticipated—two months before FY2009 began, CBO projected that the 2009 baseline deficit would be slightly lower than the 2008 deficit (for more information on the baseline, see the text box below). From 2012 to 2014, deficits declined by a similar amount—the

2014 deficit is currently projected to be about $1 trillion lower than the 2009 deficit. *Table 1* explains what factors caused this sharp increase and subsequent decrease in the deficit. Because the same policy generates different levels of spending and revenue in different fiscal years, it is not possible to say what "caused" the deficit to increase or decrease from one year to the next. However, it can be determined with precision what caused the actual deficit in any given fiscal year to be smaller or larger than what CBO had previously projected. The exact shares assigned to each category will be sensitive to the chosen starting point, however. *Table 1* uses the September 2008 projection because of the dramatic increase in the deficit relative to the projection that occurred after that date.

What is the Baseline?

Absent policy changes, budget deficits would change over time because spending and revenue levels automatically change over time. CBO baseline budget projections are used to provide a benchmark against which budgetary decisions can be made and policy proposals can be compared over the budget window. A baseline is not meant to be the best guess of future outcomes or the most desirable outcome, but a reasonable starting point for comparing policy options. The projected magnitude and path of budget deficits depends greatly on what baseline assumptions are made. These assumptions are not always realistic, but they are set in statute, limiting CBO's flexibility. Discretionary spending is generally determined annually, so various assumptions could be made about what constitutes an extension of current policy. Where discretionary spending is not determined by statutory caps, statute requires the baseline to assume an extension of current levels plus an inflation adjustment in the baseline.

CBO estimates an official 10-year *current law* baseline, which assumes that certain provisions of law will expire as scheduled, even though many of these provisions have routinely been extended in the past.[3] An example is the many tax provisions that regularly get extended in "tax extender" legislation.[4] Another example is the Medicare cuts required in law by the sustainable growth physician payment formula; Congress has enacted legislative overrides to prevent those cuts (popularly known as the "doc fix") each year since 2003.[5] CBO's current law baseline also assumes that the automatic spending cuts under the Budget Control Act will occur in future years as scheduled, although they have been reduced by subsequent legislation in the first three years they have been in place.[6]

Table 1. Contributors to the Difference between Actual Deficits and Deficits Projected Before the Financial Crisis

(billions of dollars)

	2009	2010	2011	2012	2013	2014 (projected)	Total 2009-2014
9/08 Baseline Deficit	-438	-431	-325	-126	-147	-170	-1,637
Legislative Changes	-551	-567	-736	-648	-441	-247	-3,150
—Discretionary	-47	-149	-117	-44	+75	+120	-162
—Mandatory	-295	-181	-180	-140	-93	-72	-961
—Net Interest	-4	-12	-31	-57	-78	-95	-277
—Revenue	-165	-225	-408	-407	-345	-200	-1,750
Economic Changes	-128	-124	-91	-27	-93	-42	-505
Technical Changes	-337	-168	-146	-287	0	-33	-971
Total Changes	-975	-863	-974	-960	-533	-323	-4,628
Actual Deficit	-1,413	-1,294	-1,300	-1,087	-680	-492	-6,266

Source: CRS calculations based on CBO data.

Notes: Negative sign indicates increase in the budget deficit, positive sign increases decrease in the budget deficit. CBO does not categorize the causes of discrepancies between the actual deficit and its August projection for the current FY; these discrepancies are categorized here as technical changes. CBO classifies the government's decision to transfer funds to the GSEs as a technical change. CRS has reclassified the BCA's automatic spending cuts, which came into effect when the Joint Select Committee on Deficit Reduction failed to propose legislation, from the technical changes category to the legislative changes category.

Actual budgetary outcomes can turn out differently than previously projected for three reasons— the subsequent enactment of legislation ("legislative changes" in *Table 1*), differences in CBO's projections attributable to economic forecast errors ("economic changes" in *Table 1*), and all other differences ("technical changes" in *Table 1*). For example, if more people received a tax credit or entitlement program than predicted for a given level of GDP, absent any legislative change, that would be classified as a technical change that increased the deficit. Because this table is based on the CBO baseline, policies that maintain current policy but change current law, such as extending expiring tax provisions, are classified as legislative changes.

Legislative changes since 2009 can be broken down into three broad categories, with the major changes[7] provided for each:

- *Changes that temporarily increased the deficit.* Legislation was enacted during or following the 2008-2009 recession that temporarily increased the deficit. This legislation either resulted in a one-time increase in spending (the Troubled Asset Relief Program [TARP, created by P.L. 110-343],[8] the American Reinvestment and Recovery Act [ARRA; P.L. 111-5, popularly known as the 2009 "Economic Stimulus Act"])[9] or was a temporary program that was in place for a finite period of time (extended unemployment insurance[10], payroll tax cut[11], assistance to the government sponsored enterprises [GSEs].)[12]

  Most financial stabilization outlays in the federal budget occurred within the TARP[13] or on transfers to two GSEs, Fannie Mae and Freddie Mac. These programs had a mostly one-time effect on the deficit due to improvements in financial markets and the expiration in 2010 of Treasury authority to enter into new contracts with regard to TARP and the GSEs. In 2009, outlays of $243 billion were recorded for TARP and the GSEs. In 2010 and 2011, transfers to the GSEs declined and, due to budgetary conventions, TARP recorded negative outlays that reduced the deficit.[14] CBO included transfers to the GSEs in technical, not legislative changes, although their entry into receivership was a policy decision.

  The temporary spike in spending caused by ARRA peaked in 2010 had mostly dissipated by 2012. ARRA was intended to be only a temporary boost to spending to stimulate the economy, and Congress allowed budget authority to return to near pre-ARRA levels in nominal terms.[15] (ARRA also temporarily reduced taxes, but those provisions were subsequently extended.)

  Extended unemployment insurance was in place from July 2008 through 2013.[16] Payroll taxes were temporarily reduced by two percentage points from 2011 to 2012.[17] This was the only major legislative change affecting revenues that was allowed to expire.
- *Changes that permanently reduced the deficit.* Two policy changes since September 2008 have permanently reduced the deficit—the Budget Control Act (BCA; P.L. 112-25) as amended since 2012 and the winding down of overseas contingency operations (OCO) beginning in 2009.

  Budget authority for OCO has fallen from a peak of $187 billion in 2008 to $93 billion in 2013 as overseas operations, primarily in Iraq and Afghanistan, have been scaled back. This has reduced discretionary defense spending relative to the September 2008 baseline, which assumed that such spending would increase at the rate of inflation each year.

For 2012 to 2021, the Budget Control Act (BCA; P.L. 112-25) reduced discretionary spending and mandatory spending relative to the baseline.[18] The BCA implemented spending cuts through statutory caps for defense and non-defense discretionary spending for 2012 to 2021[19] and sequestration for mandatory spending for 2013 to 2021. The BCA exempted most mandatory spending programs from sequestration and capped Medicare cuts at 2%. On the discretionary side, the BCA exempted military OCO, disaster spending, and emergency spending from the spending caps. The BCA did not provide any details as to what discretionary programs would absorb the cuts needed to adhere to the defense and non-defense caps, however, and Congress has struggled to reach a consensus on that issue each year since the BCA was enacted. Through 2014, total discretionary spending has ended up higher than envisioned under the BCA because of subsequent legislation reversing some of the BCA spending cuts and because spending in categories exempt from the caps was higher than envisioned.[20]

Overall, discretionary spending was $75 billion lower in 2013 and is projected to be $120 billion lower in 2014 than the September 2008 baseline level. The BCA cuts to mandatory spending were not large enough to offset other legislative changes that increased mandatory spending in 2013 or 2014.

- *Changes that permanently increased deficit.* Various legislative changes since September 2008 have permanently increased the deficit. The major changes involve the extension of expiring tax provisions and temporary extensions of the "doc fix."[21]

  Congress temporarily extended expiring tax provisions, including major tax cuts enacted in 2001 and 2003, numerous times. Most provisions from the 2001 and 2003 tax cuts were permanently extended in the American Taxpayer Relief Act (ATRA; P.L. 112-240) in January 2013.[22] ATRA also temporarily extended ARRA's tax cuts until 2017 and reduced revenues overall by $3.9 trillion over 10 years. On net, all legislative changes to revenues made since September 2008 have increased the budget deficit by $1,750 billion from 2009 to 2014 compared with the current law baseline. To the extent that these tax provisions involved refundable tax provisions, which are classified as mandatory spending, extending expiring provisions also increased mandatory spending. Compared with a current policy baseline, ATRA reduced the deficit because it allowed the payroll tax cut and certain provisions affecting high-income taxpayers to expire at the end of 2012. OMB estimated that the expiration of provisions affecting high-income taxpayers increased revenues by $618 billion over 10 years compared with a current policy baseline.[23]

Medicare's sustainable growth rate (SGR) system is intended to constrain Medicare payments to physicians. Congress has temporarily prevented the SGR from reducing physician payments each year since 2003 (called the "doc fix"). If Congress continues the policy that has been in place since 2003, it will permanently increase the deficit, even if there has technically been no permanent policy change so far.

All legislative changes that increase (decrease) the deficit also increase (decrease) net interest payments on the debt in future years. Combined, legislative changes to revenue, mandatory spending, and discretionary spending have increased net interest by $277 billion from 2009 to 2014.

In sum, several major legislative changes were enacted that increased the deficit between 2009 and 2012 by increasing discretionary or mandatory spending. These changes were temporary and had little effect on the deficit after 2012, except for the fact that they increased interest payments on the debt. By contrast, the (mostly permanent) extension of expiring tax cuts increased the deficit relative to current law, by $1,750 billion over six years. Policies enacted during this time that permanently reduced the deficit, notably the tapering of OCO spending and the BCA as modified, did so primarily by reducing discretionary spending. In 2013 and 2014, legislative changes reduced total discretionary spending relative to CBO's September 2008 projection, but the resulting deficit reduction was more than offset by legislative changes to mandatory spending and revenues that increased the deficit.

Economic changes, related to the recession and the sluggish recovery, added around $100 billion each year to the deficit in 2009, 2010, 2011, and 2013, and added smaller amounts in 2012 and 2014.[24] Revenues automatically rise and certain mandatory spending automatically fall as the economy moves from recession to full employment. Economists refer to these changes as "automatic stabilizers." Revenues automatically fall in a recession because taxable income falls. Recessions cause spending on certain means-tested programs, such as unemployment insurance, to automatically increase due to increased eligibility. Overall, CBO estimates that automatic stabilizers at their peak added 2.7 percentage points of GDP ($409 billion) to the budget deficit in

2010.[25] The role of automatic stabilizers has since diminished, but is still exerting some upward pressure on the deficit.

Technical changes were a major contributor to the actual deficit from 2009 to 2012, but had little effect in 2013 or 2014. These technical changes reflect the uncertainty inherent in the multitude of assumptions underlying budget projections, putting aside economic uncertainty. The joint effects of economic and technical changes illustrates that even if no legislation had been enacted since September 2008, the actual deficit would have turned out much larger than projected each year and would have increased sharply from 2008 to 2009 and remained large in 2010. There was no year between 2009 and 2014 where economic and technical changes combined exceeded legislative changes, however. Overall, the effect of legislative changes on the deficit was more than twice as large as economic and technical changes combined from 2009 to 2014, and would have been larger if assistance to the GSEs was classified as a legislative change.

How Large Are Projected Deficits Under Current Policy? What Might Change These Projections?

In the CBO baseline projection, budget deficits fall from 4.1% in 2013 to 2.8% of GDP in 2014, reaching a low of 2.6% of GDP in 2015. (The decline in 2015 is attributable to baseline assumptions and would not occur under different assumptions.) They then rise each year until reaching 4.0% of GDP in 2022. The debt held by the public declines each year until it reaches 72.4% of GDP in 2017, and then increases each year, reaching 78.1% of GDP in 2024. Long-term projections indicate that budget deficits would eventually become very large relative to GDP outside the projection window under current policy. Under a long-term projection of current policy, CBO projects deficits would exceed 10% of GDP by 2073.[26]

These projections are highly uncertain, both because of forecast errors and the underlying assumptions made about future spending and revenues. Budget projections are subject to a high degree of uncertainty—based on history, actual outcomes are likely to be much better or worse than projections, even after accounting for policy changes. Projections are often inaccurate even over short-time frames, but small changes in assumptions compound to large changes in budget projections over the long run. For that reason, forecasting errors become larger further into the future. For example, OMB estimates that the absolute average errors for its budget deficit projections are 1.4% of GDP for the next budget year and 3.6% of GDP for five years in the future.[27]

Were GDP growth lower or interest rates higher than projected, the primary deficit (i.e., deficit before interest payments) would have to be smaller in dollar terms to be sustainable, and vice versa. By historical standards, CBO's projections of economic growth over the next 10 years are relatively modest, but this is mostly because CBO projects that the labor supply will grow much more slowly than it has historically due to the aging of the population. More problematic is the role of the business cycle on budget projections. CBO's economic forecast only accounts for the short-term effects of the business cycle on the budget in the first few years of the budget window. After that, it assumes that the economy will grow at a steady rate. As a result, CBO's current projection assumes that there is no recession at any point in the next 10 years. Given that the economy has been in expansion since 2009, this projection in effect assumes that the economy will experience the longest uninterrupted economic expansion in the history of the United States. The projection would seem to account for the business cycle by assuming a growth rate that averages out the potential ebbs and flows in the business cycle. The budget has proven to be disproportionately affected by past recessions, however. In other words, were a recession to occur in the next 10 years, it would likely increase cumulative budget deficits over the course of the budget window by more than the baseline projection of steady growth, even after accounting for higher than projected growth in expansion years.

CBO's and OMB's projections assume that interest rates will remain at relatively low levels by historical standards over the next 10 years. CBO estimates that if interest rates rose to their average level from 1991 to 2000, the budget deficit would be an average of $144 billion higher per year over the next 10 years. If interest rates rose to their average level from 1981 to 1990, the budget deficit would be an average of $627 billion higher per year over the next 10 years.[28]

Besides forecast errors, the baseline projection is based on a number of policy assumptions when alternative assumptions could be employed that would be equally valid. Changing these assumptions would increase or decrease deficit projections. The following examples involve ambiguity about how to define current policy (in contrast to projections about future legislative changes, not meant to be captured in the baseline).

- *War spending*—The baseline assumption that current discretionary spending levels (adjusted for inflation) will be maintained is likely to prove inaccurate when circumstances are expected to change significantly. An example is discretionary spending on overseas contingency operations (OCO). A planned reduction in the American troop presence in Iraq and Afghanistan may reduce future OCO spending from current levels (which are already at half of their peak 2008 level), but the baseline assumes that 2014 spending levels will continue. On the other hand, these projections also assume that no new military conflict will require additional budgetary resources over the next 10 years.
- *Disaster spending*—Like OCO spending, disaster spending is extrapolated at current year levels adjusted for inflation. Disaster spending varies significantly from year to year, however. In some years, disaster spending is minimal; in years with major disasters, it can exceed $50 billion. Disaster spending is limited by the BCA by a formula based on a 10-year average; however, the BCA also allows any discretionary spending to be designated as emergency spending. For any particular year, an amount based on the prior 10 years is arguably reasonable, but, based on historical experience, disaster spending is likely to significantly exceed that amount at least once in the next 10 years.
- *Emergency spending designation*—For most categories of discretionary spending that are exempt from the statutory caps, the BCA defines eligible spending by budget account or limits the amount. One notable exception is emergency spending, which is designated by Congress and the BCA does not constrain. In effect, any type or amount of discretionary spending can be designated as emergency spending. To date, the emergency spending designation has been used in one out of the three years that caps have been in effect—$41.6 billion in 2013, related to Hurricane Sandy relief. Going forward, CBO assumes emergency spending will be zero, but any amount is possible under current law.
- *SGR ("doc fix")*—As discussed above, Congress has enacted the "doc fix" on a temporary basis, rather than repealing the SGR. As a result, the CBO baseline assumes that the SGR will be in effect in future years. If Congress continues to prevent the SGR from coming into effect, budget deficits would be $148 billion higher over 10 years.

- *Expiring tax provisions ("extenders")*—Many provisions of the tax code are scheduled to expire under current law. Congress routinely extends some, but not all, of these provisions, often for one year at a time. If all expiring provisions were permanently extended, budget deficits would be $1.1 trillion higher over 10 years.[29]

Unforeseen circumstances and inaccurate assumptions played a major role in the movement from projected baseline surpluses to actual deficits in the last decade. [30] Historically, emergencies and other unforeseen events have typically been deficit financed. The baseline could not anticipate events, such as war in Iraq and Afghanistan, Hurricane Katrina, and two recessions, that were major contributors to last decade's budget deficits. Furthermore, baseline assumptions (some of which are set in statute) that were unrepresentative of past events—such as assumptions that discretionary spending would grow only at the rate of inflation (in years without statutory caps) and tax provisions would expire as scheduled—proved unrepresentative of future events, and this caused baseline deficit projections to repeatedly undershoot. This experience raises the question of the utility of relying on projections, particularly over longer budget windows. Another conclusion is that if budget plans do not use realistic assumptions or build in assumptions about unforeseen contingencies, they are unlikely to prove accurate.

In addition to ambiguity about how to best capture current policy in a baseline, it is useful to remember that, on a conceptual level, the baseline does not attempt to account for policy changes even if they are likely or predictable. For example, Congress has intervened to prevent the full effects of the Budget Control Act's automatic spending cuts from occurring each year (although it has not eliminated them entirely). One might conclude it is not only possible, but probable, that future Congresses may similarly intervene to reduce these spending cuts. Because the baseline measures current law, it assumes that those cuts will be implemented in their entirety.

To account for some of these issues caused by baseline assumptions, CBO also presents an Alternative Fiscal Scenario that assumes that the doc fix and expiring tax provisions do not expire and that the BCA's automatic spending reductions do not come into effect. Under the Alternative Fiscal Scenario, the budget deficit continues to rise and peaks at 5.1% of GDP in 2022 and the debt held by the public rises as a share of GDP each year, reaching 86.7% of GDP by 2024. Deficits reach 10% of GDP in 2032 and the debt held by the public reaches 100% of GDP by 2029.

How Much Deficit Reduction Is Necessary?

There is no clear answer to the question of how much the deficit should be reduced because the targeted amount of deficit reduction depends on the policy goal.

- A balanced budget could be pursued so that the government would have a neutral effect on the national saving rate (by accounting identity, budget deficits reduce the national saving rate).[31] Since the United States has a low national saving rate relative to other countries and relative to domestic investment needs, it could be argued that the government should at least not continue to reduce the national saving rate by running budget deficits in the future.
- If the policy goal were for the government to increase the national saving rate or reduce the federal debt in dollar terms, then the government could target a budget surplus.
- A desire to achieve generational equity, so that government spending on present age cohorts was not disproportionately paid for by future age cohorts, would require large budget surpluses today because of the interaction between an aging population and the pay-as-you-go structure of elderly entitlement programs.
- Some economists call for a balanced structural budget (i.e., a budget that would be balanced if the economy were at full employment), which would allow for modest deficits in downturns and budget surpluses in boom times. This would avoid deficit reduction during a recession that added contractionary pressures on the economy. For 2012, a structurally balanced budget would have allowed for an actual deficit of about 2.3% of GDP.[32]
- A less ambitious policy goal would be to place fiscal policy on a sustainable path in the medium to long term. History demonstrates that budget deficits can be sustained indefinitely as long as they are small enough that government debt does not continuously grow more quickly than GDP. The budget is not projected to be on a sustainable path under current policy in the long term because the debt held by the public would continuously grow more quickly than GDP. Economists view this as unsustainable because it would imply that an ever-growing portion of national income would be needed to meet interest payments. Under the baseline, the debt would reach 79% of GDP in 2024 and

> 106% of GDP in 2039. Under the Alternative Fiscal Scenario, the debt grows modestly relative to GDP in the short run and reaches 163% of GDP by 2039. As long as investors remain willing to finance large deficits, there is no barrier to the debt continuing to grow relative to GDP, and there has been no difficulty in financing it to date.[33]

Because deficits are projected to continue to grow in the long run, growing reductions in spending or increases in taxes would be required over time to maintain sustainability. Cutting spending or raising taxes sooner rather than later would reduce the need for future changes. CBO projects that spending would need to be cut or revenues increased by 1.8% of GDP immediately and permanently to stabilize the debt-to-GDP ratio over the next 75 years, or 7.4% of GDP under the alternative fiscal scenario.[34] Today's debt levels, high by historical standards, leave policymakers less room to maneuver to cope with future challenges—both anticipated, such as the retirement of the baby boomers, and unanticipated.

How Quickly Should the Deficit Be Reduced?

The state of the economy is an important factor to consider in determining the desired timing of deficit reduction. All else equal, mainstream economic theory predicts that reducing the deficit would have a contractionary effect on GDP in the short run, whether through tax increases or spending reductions (which is a component of GDP). During a period of robust economic growth, that contractionary effect would be more easily offset by other sectors of the economy, and the expansion would likely be sustained. During a period of high unemployment, reducing the budget deficit would be expected to make unemployment higher (or fall more slowly) than would otherwise be the case, all else equal. The economy is now closer to full employment than it has been since the recession, but there is considerable disagreement among economists as to how close and growth has not yet been robust.[35]

On the other hand, deficit reduction will eventually be needed to achieve sustainability, and given that the effect on the economy is proportional to the size of the deficit reduction, it could be argued that avoiding unwanted contractionary effects suggests a gradual approach to deficit reduction. Furthermore, policy changes can be phased in such a way that they have little contractionary effect in the short run. Waiting until deficits have become larger leaves less latitude for phasing in changes.

The U.S. fiscal outlook is not a purely long-term issue, however—deficits are already above average today, and while projected deficits outside the 10-year budget window are larger than today's deficits, they are also more uncertain. Deficits are also a long-term issue in the sense that most observers believe fundamental reforms to outlays and revenues would be necessary to put the budget on a sustainable path; however, any delay to implementing those changes increases the eventual budgetary cost of returning to a sustainable fiscal path, all else equal.

The deficit is a long-term issue in that any negative economic consequences from running large deficits have been minor to date, but there is the risk that the deficit's effect on the economy could become negative at any time. Although economic theory suggests that larger deficits provided a stimulative boost to the economy during the recent recession by partially offsetting the contraction of private spending, continued deficits would be expected to eventually have a negative effect on the economy. At some point, the economy is expected to return to full employment (i.e., practically all existing labor and capital resources are in use). When it does, government budget deficits are expected to "crowd out," or compete with, private-investment spending in the standard macroeconomic model. Setting aside foreign capital flows for the moment, borrowing can only be financed through saving, and government borrowing competes with business borrowing for the same pool of national saving. By increasing the demands on that pool of national saving, government borrowing pushes up the cost of all borrowing through higher interest rates, causing businesses to finance less capital spending than they otherwise would. Business borrowing finances capital spending on plant and equipment, and lower capital spending results in lower potential gross domestic product, and hence lower future national income, than would otherwise occur.

The financial crisis and Great Recession led to a marked decline in private-investment spending and increase in private saving. Both of these factors reduced the potential for large government deficits to crowd out private-investment spending. Low interest rates since the recession began support the view that the deficit caused little crowding out to occur.

With international capital mobility, borrowing can also be financed by foreign saving. In the standard macroeconomic model with perfect capital mobility, the boost in aggregate spending from the stimulus would cause the trade deficit to rise as foreign capital is attracted to higher domestic interest rates. Net foreign borrowing is equivalent to the trade deficit because one country can borrow from the rest of the world only if it imports more than it exports. The availability of foreign credit would avoid the crowding out of domestic capital investment. But the boost to aggregate spending from the budget deficit would be negated (or "crowded out") by the higher trade deficit (in the form of lower exports, higher imports, or both). The United States relies heavily on foreign borrowing, and this is another reason that large budget deficits could be less effective at stimulating the economy. Since the recession began, the trade deficit has fallen substantially, so a problem of crowding out from the trade deficit is not apparent at this time.

Despite the significant decline in the budget deficit since 2012, crowding out and higher interest rates will likely become a more pressing issue as the economy returns to full employment because of the anticipated increase in business investment back to historically normal levels, particularly if the increase in private saving following the recession proves not to be permanent. If that is the case, the decline in the trade deficit may reverse. Interest rates have already increased modestly as the economy has strengthened, although they remain low compared with those prevailing in recent decades.

Policy Options for Deficit Reduction

Budget deficits can be reduced through cuts in spending, higher taxes, or a combination of both.[36] Plans to reduce the deficit that are narrowly targeted require commensurately larger spending cuts or tax increases to targeted programs or provisions. To that end, deficit reduction proposals can start with the observation that Social Security, Medicare, net interest (which cannot be changed), and defense discretionary make up almost two-thirds of total spending. *Figure 1* compares the projected deficit to overall spending and revenues in 2014. It shows that the deficit is about two-fifths the size of all non-interest spending outside of Social Security, Medicare, and defense discretionary. It is about one-sixth the size of total revenues.

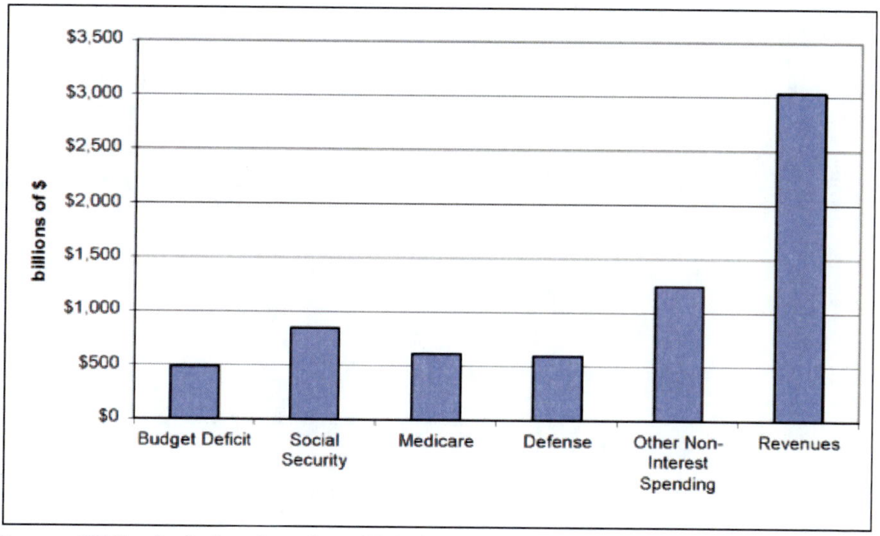

Source: CRS calculations based on CBO data.

Note: Budget deficit, spending, and revenues for 2014 are projected based on the CBO baseline.

Figure 1. Selected Data from 2014 Federal Budget (billions of dollars).

Budget deficits are the result of the shortfall between spending and revenue. In 2009, spending reached its highest share of GDP since 1945 and revenues reached their lowest share of GDP since 1950. As seen in *Figure 2*, from 1946 to 2008, outlays averaged 19.6% of GDP and were generally below 20% of GDP until 1975, above 20% of GDP from 1975 to 1996, and below 20% of GDP from 1997 to 2005. From 2009 to 2011, outlays averaged 24.1% of GDP. From 1946 to 2008, revenues averaged 17.8% of GDP, showing no long-term upward or downward trend from 1952 to 2007. Revenues were at least 17% of GDP in each year during that period except for 1955, 1959, 2003, and 2004, when they were between 16% and 17%. From 2009 to 2012, revenues were below 16% of GDP.

Over the next 10 years, revenues are projected to be near their historical average at 18.1% of GDP. Outlays are projected to be 21.5% of GDP, above their historical average of 19.6% of GDP and comparable to their level from 1975 to 1996. However, the composition of outlays is projected to be significantly different, as discussed below.

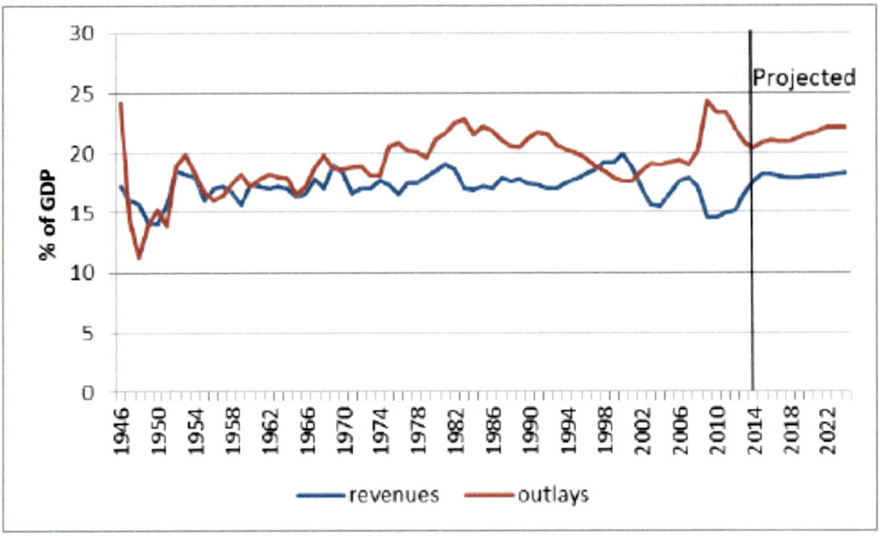

Source: OMB and CBO.

Figure 2. Federal Revenues and Outlays, Historical and Baseline Projection. (1946-2024)

Just as recent deficits are the combination of all past outlay and revenue decisions, returning the budget to balance would be difficult without a combination of outlay and revenue changes. For instance, to return the budget to balance while maintaining baseline revenue levels would require that outlays decline to a share of GDP last seen in the early 1970s. Likewise, to balance the budget while maintaining baseline outlay levels would require revenues to rise to their highest share of GDP ever.

Federal Spending

Total spending has fallen from an average of 24% of GDP from 2009 to 2011 to 21% of GDP in 2013. It is projected to rise to 22% of GDP from 2020 to 2024 under current policy. From 1946 to 2008, there were only three years when outlays were above 23% of GDP. Spending rises under the baseline projection despite discretionary spending falling to its lowest share of GDP since data were first collected because mandatory spending and net interest on the federal debt are projected to grow relative to GDP. The projected increase in net interest is due to the growth in the federal debt and the return to more normal interest rates from the current below-average rates.

Discretionary Spending

Discretionary spending has fallen from 12.3% of GDP in 1962 to a projected 6.8% of GDP in 2014. Discretionary spending was at high levels relative to GDP from 2009 to 2012, but not historically high levels since data were first available in 1962, as seen in *Figure 3*. Over time, the two components of discretionary spending, defense and non-defense, have followed different paths. Defense discretionary spending was lower from 2009 to 2012 than it was in all but two years from 1962 to 1992 as a share of GDP. From 1963 to 2001, defense discretionary spending generally fell relative to GDP, but rose in nominal dollars. It then began to grow, when overseas military operations expanded. In 2014, defense discretionary spending is projected to fall to its lowest share of GDP since 2002.

Non-defense discretionary spending has shown no long-term upward or downward trend relative to GDP—except for an elevated period from 1975 to 1983, it has always stayed within 3% to 4% of GDP. Over the late 1990s, it fell to its lowest level of GDP since data have been collected, and then rose from that low base in the 2000s. It was above its long-term average from 2009 to 2012, but still below the levels prevalent from 1975 to 1981. Since 2009, much of the growth in nondefense discretionary spending was a result of the 2009 stimulus (ARRA). Most discretionary spending provided under this act was completed by 2011. In 2014, non-defense discretionary spending is projected to fall back to the historically low levels of the 1990s, which is well below its share of GDP before the 1990s.

In the CBO baseline, discretionary spending declines significantly relative to GDP over the next 10 years to its lowest share of GDP ever since data were first collected in 1962, as shown in *Figure 3*. The baseline, based on current law, assumes that discretionary spending will adhere to the levels set in the Budget Control Act (BCA) through 2021 and discretionary spending not subject to the caps (notably, OCO) will rise at the rate of inflation. In long-term projections, CBO assumes discretionary spending will remain at its 2024 share of GDP. Because discretionary spending is held constant, it becomes a smaller share of spending over time and therefore does not contribute to the growth of the long-term budget deficit. If assumed instead that discretionary spending remained at its current share of GDP, non-interest spending would be 1.5 percentage points higher annually and long-term deficits would be even larger.

Discretionary spending fell in nominal terms (i.e., not adjusted for inflation) each year from 2011 to 2014. From 1963 to 2010, discretionary spending fell in nominal terms in only four years, most recently in 1996. Adjusted for inflation, both defense and non-defense spending fell in real terms each year from 2011 to 2013, and they are projected to continue falling each year through 2018. The decline is caused by the decline in the BCA caps in real terms and, through 2014, in OCO spending. This contrasts to the significant growth in discretionary spending that occurred from 2000 to 2010, as shown in *Table 2*.

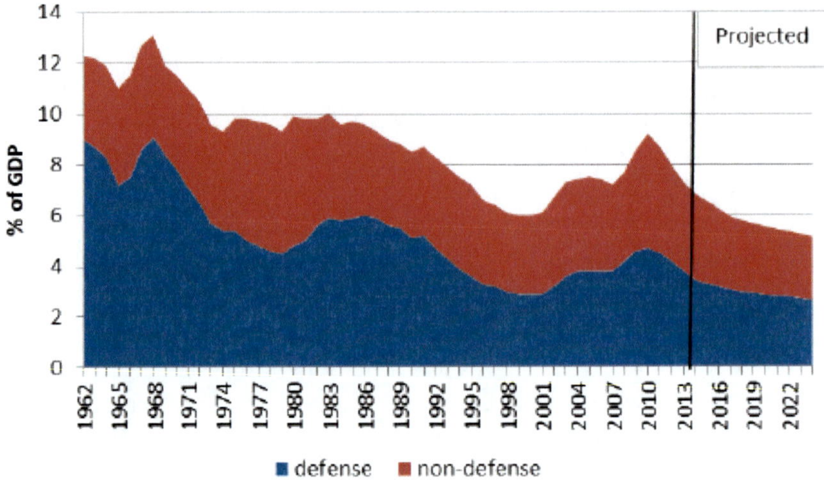

Source: OMB and CBO.

Note: Figure assumes BCA's automatic spending cuts are implemented and current levels of OCO and disaster spending are maintained, adjusted for inflation.

Figure 3. Discretionary Spending, Historical and Projected in the Baseline. (1962-2024)

Table 2. Average Annual Real Growth Rates of Discretionary Spending Outlays

(actual and CBO baseline, adjusted for inflation)

	Defense	Non-Defense
2000-2008	5.1%	3.0%
2009-2010	5.7%	11.4%
2011-2014	-4.8%	-4.6%
2015-2021	-0.2%	-1.0%

Source: CRS calculations based on OMB and CBO data.

Notes: Data for 2000 to 2013 are actual; data for 2014 to 2021 assume that spending cuts under the BCA will occur as scheduled, with OCO spending maintained in real terms at 2014 levels.

One macroeconomic implication of reducing discretionary spending is that most federal spending on physical capital (e.g., infrastructure) and human capital (e.g., education) is located in the discretionary portion of the budget. Economic theory predicts that a lower future capital stock would result in a smaller economy from what it otherwise would be in the long term, all else equal.[37]

To achieve further deficit reduction through discretionary spending would involve reducing discretionary spending even lower as a share of GDP than the all-time low already achieved under the BCA. By 2030, if discretionary spending were reduced to zero, there would still be a deficit in the extended baseline scenario. For defense, the timing and magnitude of any potential drawdown in overseas military operations could cause military spending to decline relative to the baseline, but traditionally such changes have not been motivated by the desire for deficit reduction. Even if current operations are reduced, future geopolitical events could require military personnel to be deployed elsewhere in the next 10 years, so the baseline does not necessarily overestimate future defense spending.

Mandatory Spending

Unlike discretionary spending, mandatory spending has grown as a share of GDP since 1962. Net of offsetting receipts, it doubled relative to GDP from 1962 to 1975, increasing from 4.7% to 9.4% of GDP. It then fluctuated in a range of 8.7% to 10.4% of GDP from 1975 to 2007, peaking in recession years in part because of automatic stabilizers. It peaked at 14.5% of GDP in 2009, marking its highest share of GDP since data were first compiled in 1962. Mandatory spending has fallen as a share of GDP since, but has remained above its pre-crisis share of GDP.

In contrast to discretionary spending, mandatory spending is projected to continue to grow faster than inflation and exceed 13% of GDP over the next 10 years under current policy. Since 1962, mandatory spending fell in nominal terms in only one year, 2010; outside of TARP and deposit insurance, which recorded negative outlays that year, all other mandatory spending grew in 2010.

Outside of health and retirement programs, outlays on other mandatory programs are projected to decline relative to GDP over the next 10 years. As the economy improves, "automatic stabilizer" spending has declined significantly: spending on income security programs more than doubled in nominal terms between 2007 and 2010, but is projected to decline from $438 billion in 2010 to $219 billion in 2014. Over its 75-year projection, CBO assumes that other mandatory spending will fall from 2.7% of GDP in 2013 to 0.8% of GDP by

2088. Since data were collected in 1974, it has never been lower than 1.9% of GDP.

Over the long term, however, the upward trend in mandatory spending in the past and future is dominated by entitlement spending on the elderly (Social Security, Medicare, and Medicaid), which accounted for about three-quarters of total mandatory spending in 2010. Social Security has risen from 3.7% of GDP in 1974 to 4.9% of GDP in 2013, its highest share of GDP ever. Major mandatory health programs (Medicare, Medicaid, the Children's Health Insurance Program, and health insurance exchange subsidies, net of offsetting receipts) rose from 1% of GDP in 1974 to 5% of GDP in 2011, its highest share of GDP ever, before falling to 4.6% of GDP in 2013.

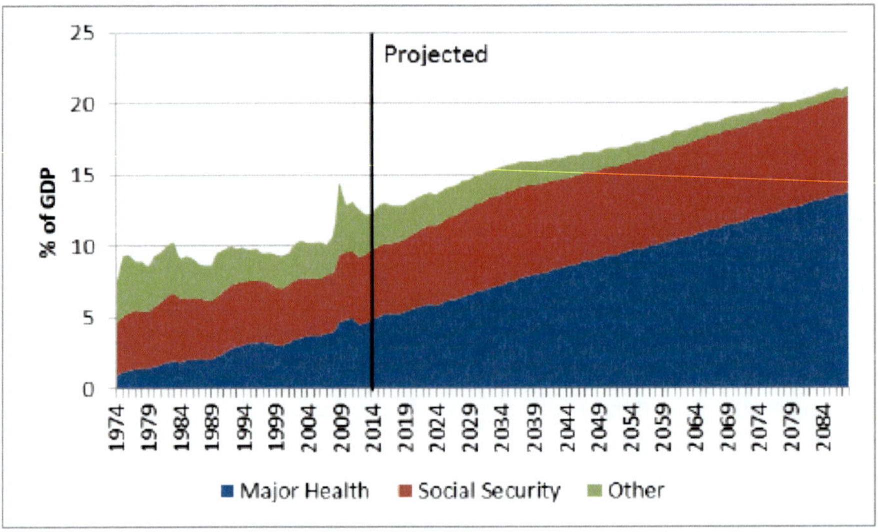

Source: CBO, Long-Term Budget Outlook, Supplementary Data, July 2014.
Notes: Projection using CBO's Extended Baseline.

Figure 4. Mandatory Spending, Historic and Projected. (1974-2084)

Within the 10-year baseline, Social Security and major health spending each exceed total discretionary spending for the first time. In long-term budget projections, rising budget deficits are driven primarily by the growth in entitlement programs for the elderly, particularly health spending. Social Security outlays are projected to rise from 4.9% of GDP today to 6.3% of GDP in 2039, and federal health outlays (mainly on Medicare and Medicaid) are projected to rise from 4.9% today to 8.0% of GDP in 2039. By 2066, outlays on

Social Security and health programs would exceed projected total revenues in 2014 as a share of GDP.

In long-term projections, health spending per capita is projected to continue to grow faster than GDP per capita because it has historically grown much more quickly. If health spending per capita grew at the same rate as GDP per capita (technically, this is referred to as an excess cost growth rate of zero), one-third of the increase in federal health spending would be avoided through 2039, although spending would still grow somewhat because of demographic changes— namely, the retirement of the baby boomers—that increased the number of recipients. *Figure 5* illustrates that if there was zero excess cost growth over the next 75 years, spending on major health programs would decline from 14% of GDP to 7.7% of GDP in 2089. The difference between the two is significantly larger than the baseline primary deficit (2.6% of GDP) in 2089. Therefore, if health spending were to grow at the rate of GDP instead, the budget would be on a sustainable path.

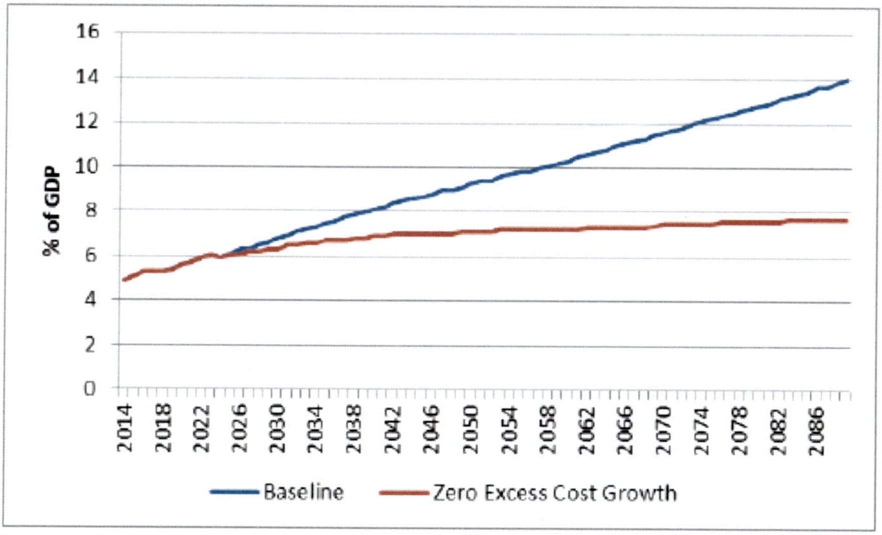

Source: Congressional Budget Office, Long-Term Budget Outlook, Supplementary Data, July 2014.

Figure 5. Projected Spending on Major Health Programs: CBO Baseline vs Zero Excess Cost Growth. (2014 to 2089)

The growth in elderly entitlement spending makes deficits unsustainably large in the long run. In part, the link between entitlement spending and deficits is driven by the assumptions that go into these projections—other spending is assumed to gradually fall relative to GDP in the long run, revenues are projected to gradually rise relative to GDP because of bracket creep, while health spending per capita is projected to continue to grow faster than GDP per capita. Restraining the future growth rate of elderly entitlement spending would not result in significant deficit reduction in the short run, however. Most proposals to reform elderly entitlement programs would generate significant budgetary savings in the long run, but little budgetary savings in the short run, partly because most proposals exempt current retirees from reform and partly because the savings from these changes would compound over time. For example, immediately reducing excess cost growth for federal health spending to zero would reduce federal spending by 2% of GDP after 20 Mandatory spending could be reduced by restricting benefits or eligibility. For retirement programs, it is straightforward to do so through a change in the benefit formula. For health programs, it is less straightforward, and there is a lack of consensus on how excess cost growth, which has persisted for decades, can be effectively minimized. On a positive note, excess cost growth has shown a downward trend over time. However, CBO's projections already assume the decline will continue, and it still results in an unsustainably large budget deficit.

Revenues

In 2009 and 2010, revenues were at historically low shares of GDP across all major categories— individual income taxes were at their lowest share of GDP since 1950, corporate income taxes were at their lowest share of GDP since the 1930s, social insurance receipts were at their lowest share of GDP since the 1970s, and excise taxes were at their lowest share of GDP since 1934, the first year for which data are available. Total revenues remained at historically low shares of GDP in 2011 and 2012, as shown in *Figure 2*. In recent years, most revenues have come from the individual income tax and social insurance categories. In 2013, revenue as a share of GDP returned closer to historically average levels because of the economic recovery and because of the expiration of the payroll tax cut and certain provisions from the 2001 and 2003 tax cuts.[38]

Revenues in the CBO baseline are projected to equal about 18% of GDP from 2015 on, around their historical average. Total revenues would gradually increase relative to GDP over the next 10 years due to the improvement in the economy (initially) and "real bracket creep," returning to their historical average around 2014. "Real bracket creep" refers to the fact that the same tax structure generates more revenue relative to GDP when incomes rise. Bracket creep does not lead to a significant increase in revenues relative to GDP over a 10-year projection, but it does over a 75-year projection. In CBO's Long-Term Budget Outlook, projected revenues increase by 1.8 percentage points to 19.4% of GDP as a result of bracket creep in 2039. By 2089, revenues would reach 23.9% of GDP, which would represent their highest share of GDP ever. Revenues also increase by 0.3 percentage points by 2039 because it is assumed that temporary provisions will be allowed to expire, although many are routinely extended. An argument could be made that current law does not represent current policy in long-term projections, because current law would make revenues reach an unprecedented share of GDP. If argued instead that the revenues equal to current share of GDP represented current policy, then the long-term fiscal gap would be much larger because revenues would not rise in tandem with spending as a share of GDP.

If policymakers decided to increase revenue to reduce the deficit, five broad choices are often discussed:[39]

- redesigning the structure of the tax system;
- adding new revenue sources, such as a carbon tax or a value added tax (VAT);
- increasing existing taxes;
- "broadening the tax base" by eliminating tax expenditures (deductions, exemptions, and credits); or
- allowing tax cuts to expire as scheduled.

Redesigning the tax system or adding new revenue sources could theoretically improve economic efficiency and might be more appealing to some than increasing existing taxes, but in practice, compensating those made worse off from these changes may result in those policies raising little additional revenue. Generally, economists favor eliminating tax expenditures over raising marginal tax rates on efficiency grounds, although some specific expenditures may promote economic efficiency. Tax expenditures have also been criticized on the grounds of equity and complexity.[40]

End Notes

[1] All budget data presented in this report are from Congressional Budget Office, Updated Budget Projections, April 2014, Congressional Budget Office, Budget and Economic Outlook, February 2014 (hereafter referred to as "CBO baseline"), Congressional Budget Office, The

2013 Long-Term Budget Outlook, July 2014, or Office of Management and Budget, FY2015 Budget of the U.S. Government, March 2014 (hereafter referred to as "President's Budget"). The budget deficit is the excess of outlays over revenues in a given year, broadly similar to the amount borrowed from the public that year. The publicly held debt is the accumulation of all past borrowing from the public. The gross debt is the publicly held debt and the intragovernmental debt (the debt that one part of the federal government borrows from another part, mainly government trust funds). All references to years are to fiscal years, unless otherwise noted. This report primarily focuses on CBO's projections because of its role for Congress, but this analysis also applies to budget projections made by OMB and others.

[2] Expressing budget data as a percentage of GDP is most appropriate for making comparisons over extended periods of time because it allows the relative size of those amounts to be consistently compared. Dollar figures are not appropriate because of inflation, which means that a dollar has a smaller amount of purchasing power over time, and because as the economy has become larger, there are more resources available to finance spending through borrowing or taxes.

[3] Some expiring mandatory spending programs are assumed to continue under the baseline. According to CBO, "The Deficit Control Act specifies some exceptions. For example, spending programs whose authorizations are set to expire are assumed to continue if they have outlays of more than $50 million in the current year and were established at the time of or before the enactment of the Balanced Budget Act of 1997. Programs established after that law was enacted are not automatically assumed to continue but are considered individually in consultation with the budget committees." Congressional Budget Office, Budget and Economic Outlook, January 2012, p. 11.

[4] For more information, see CRS Report R43124, Expired and Expiring Temporary Tax Provisions ("Tax Extenders"), by Molly F. Sherlock.

[5] For more information, see CRS Report R40907, Medicare Physician Payment Updates and the Sustainable Growth Rate (SGR) System, by Jim Hahn.

[6] For more information, see CRS Report R43411, The Budget Control Act of 2011: Legislative Changes to the Law and Their Budgetary Effects, by Mindy R. Levit.

[7] The Affordable Care Act (P.L. 111-148) was a major legislative change that permanently increased taxes and mandatory spending, but it is not highlighted below because its effect on the deficit was relatively modest until 2013 and 2014, when CBO estimated it would reduce the deficit. The effect on the deficit was modest until then because these changes were offsetting and gradually phased in.

[8] For more information, see CRS Report R41427, Troubled Asset Relief Program (TARP): Implementation and Status, by Baird Webel.

[9] ARRA resulted in a one-time increase in budget authority that was outlayed over several fiscal years. For more information, see CRS Report R40537, American Recovery and Reinvestment Act of 2009 (P.L. 111-5): Summary and Legislative History, by Clinton T. Brass et al.

[10] For more information, see CRS Report R41508, Expiring Unemployment Insurance Provisions, by Katelin P. Isaacs.

[11] For more information, see CRS Report R41648, Social Security: Temporary Payroll Tax Reduction, by Dawn Nuschler.

[12] For more information, see CRS Report RL34661, Fannie Mae's and Freddie Mac's Financial Problems, by N. Eric Weiss.

[13] TARP was created by the Emergency Economic Stabilization Act (P.L. 110-343).

[14] Reductions in TARP's projected lifetime cost led to negative outlays in 2010 and 2011 to compensate for what proved in hindsight to be too large an estimate of its cost in 2009.

[15] In 2008, before ARRA was enacted, non-defense discretionary budget authority was $494 billion. In 2009, it was $803 billion, but in 2011, it was $511 billion.

[16] For more information, see CRS Report R41508, Expiring Unemployment Insurance Provisions, by Katelin P. Isaacs.

[17] For more information, see CRS Report R41648, Social Security: Temporary Payroll Tax Reduction, by Dawn Nuschler.

[18] Discretionary spending is spending controlled by the appropriations process. Mandatory spending is controlled by other laws and includes entitlement spending.

[19] In 2012, there were security and non-security caps instead.

[20] See CRS Report R43411, The Budget Control Act of 2011: Legislative Changes to the Law and Their Budgetary Effects, by Mindy R. Levit.

[21] For more information, see CRS Report R40907, Medicare Physician Payment Updates and the Sustainable Growth Rate (SGR) System, by Jim Hahn.

[22] See CRS Report R42894, An Overview of the Tax Provisions in the American Taxpayer Relief Act of 2012, by Margot L. Crandall-Hollick.

[23] Office of Management and Budget, "American Taxpayer Relief Act Reduces Deficits by $737 billion," blog, January 1, 2013, http://www.whitehouse.gov/blog/2013/01/01/american-taxpayer-relief-act-reduces-deficits-737-billion.

[24] In September 2008, CBO was projecting that the economy would grow at a modest rate in 2008 and 2009. Instead, the economy sharply contracted.

[25] Congressional Budget Office, The Effects of Automatic Stabilizers on the Federal Budget as of 2013, March 2013.

[26] Long-term budget data can be found in Congressional Budget Office, The Long-Term Budget Outlook, July 2014.

[27] Office of Management and Budget, FY2015 Budget of the U.S. Government: Analytical Perspectives, March 2014, p. 20.

[28] Congressional Budget Office, How Different Future Interest Rates Would Affect Budget Deficits, Blog post, March 27, 2013, available at http://www.cbo.gov/publication/44024.

[29] While tax provisions are assumed in the baseline to expire as scheduled, it is assumed that major mandatory spending programs will continue past their expiration date.

[30] For more information, see CRS Report R41134, The Impact of Major Legislation on Budget Deficits: 2001 to 2010, by Marc Labonte and Margot L. Crandall-Hollick.

[31] In simple terms, saving is measured by the excess of income over spending. When the government's outlays exceed its revenues, it must borrow from the public to finance the difference, and it has a negative saving rate.

[32] Congressional Budget Office, The Effects of Automatic Stabilizers on the Federal Budget as of 2013, March 2013.

[33] Economic effects of an unsustainable budget deficit are discussed in CRS Report R40770, The Sustainability of the Federal Budget Deficit: Market Confidence and Economic Effects, by Marc Labonte.

[34] Congressional Budget Office, The Long-Term Budget Outlook, September 2013, p. 117. Economists call this concept the "fiscal gap." Because the debt to GDP ratio rises continuously over long-term projections, a longer time period leads to a larger fiscal gap estimate.

[35] See CRS Report R43476, Returning to Full Employment: What Do the Indicators Tell Us?, by Marc Labonte.

[36] CBO estimates that the budget would still be in deficit at full employment, so there is a limit to how much higher economic growth could reduce the deficit.

[37] About half of federal spending on physical capital is for defense, and reduced defense capital spending may not have the same economic effects as reduced non-defense capital spending.

[38] See CRS Report R42894, An Overview of the Tax Provisions in the American Taxpayer Relief Act of 2012, by Margot L. Crandall-Hollick.

[39] For a further analysis, see CRS Report R41641, Reducing the Budget Deficit: Tax Policy Options, by Molly F. Sherlock.

[40] For more information, see CRS Report RL33641, Tax Expenditures: Trends and Critiques, by Thomas L. Hungerford.

In: Federal Deficits and Debt
Editor: Jamie Malone
ISBN: 978-1-53610-268-0

Chapter 3

THE SUSTAINABILITY OF THE FEDERAL BUDGET DEFICIT: MARKET CONFIDENCE AND ECONOMIC EFFECTS*

Marc Labonte

SUMMARY

The budget deficit has exceeded $1 trillion since 2009. Combined with a shrinking economy, deficits increased the publicly held federal debt by over 30 percentage points of GDP between 2008 and 2012. Deficits of this size are not sustainable in the long run because the federal debt cannot indefinitely grow faster than output. Over time, a greater and greater share of national income would be devoted to servicing the debt, until eventually the government would be forced to finance the debt through money creation or default.

The current policy debate on the "fiscal cliff" occurring at the end of 2012 has raised the question of whether a deficit of the current magnitude is manageable and what risks it poses to the economy. Since deficit reduction could have a contractionary effect on the economy in the short run at a time when the economy is still fragile, restoring fiscal sustainability poses another set of risks that must be balanced against the risks of continuing an unsustainably large deficit. This report will evaluate sustainability issues.

---

* This is an edited, reformatted and augmented version of a Congressional Research Service publication, R40770, dated December 14, 2012.

Although the debt cannot persistently rise relative to GDP, it can rise for a time. It is hard to predict at what point bond holders would deem it to be unsustainable. A few other advanced economies have debt-to-GDP ratios higher than that of the United States. Some of those countries in Europe have recently seen their financing costs rise to the point that they are unable to finance their deficits solely through private markets. But Japan has the highest debt-to-GDP ratio of any advanced economy, and it has continued to be able to finance its debt at extremely low costs.

If investors on balance deemed the debt to be unsustainable, the yields and the cost of credit default swaps on Treasury securities would be expected to rise. Instead, both are currently low. This may seem surprising, given that the debt is currently growing more rapidly than output and is projected to continue to do so under current policy. The willingness of bond holders to finance the federal debt at low interest rates in light of these projections suggests that they believe that policy changes will eventually be made to place the federal debt on a sustainable path. This belief could change at any time; if it did, the experience of foreign countries suggests that the effects on the economy and financial markets could be severe. A failure to raise the debt limit or a ratings downgrade of U.S. debt by a credit rating agency are two events that have been seen as potential catalysts for a change in investor sentiment, although the downgrade when the debt nearly reached its statutory limit in 2011 did not result in higher yields.

According to standard macroeconomic theory, large deficits have temporarily boosted overall spending at a time when there is significant slack in the economy. Once private investment demand recovers, a large deficit would be expected to "crowd out" private investment spending. By accounting identity, domestic investment spending equals national saving plus net borrowing from abroad. The budget deficit has been equal to about half of private saving over the last three years. Even before the increase in the deficit, national saving was insufficient to finance domestic investment spending, and the United States was borrowing from abroad at unprecedented rates, peaking at about 6% of GDP. (Borrowing from abroad has since fallen by half, but remains relatively high.) To sustain large deficits, the economy will require some combination of higher private saving, lower investment, and higher borrowing from abroad. Some economists have argued that borrowing much more than 6% of GDP from abroad is unrealistic, and the already heavy U.S. reliance on borrowing from abroad makes the maintenance of a large budget deficit even less sustainable.

INTRODUCTION

The federal budget deficit totaled $1.4 trillion in FY2009, which was the first time it ever topped $1 trillion. It remained over $1 trillion for the next three fiscal years. The government's ability to finance a budget deficit depends on the size of the economy. For this reason, and to compare the deficit to historical or foreign deficits, it is more meaningful to measure the deficit relative to gross domestic product (GDP). By this measure, the deficits since 2009 are unusual but not unprecedented. The deficit was above 10% of GDP in 2009, 9% of GDP in 2010, 8% of GDP in 2011, and 7% of GDP in 2012. Seven previous times in U.S. history the federal budget deficit has exceeded 10% of GDP, these being during or following the Civil War (1865), World War I (1918, 1919), and World War II (1942-1945). Before 2009, it had not exceeded 7% of GDP since 1946.

Federal budget deficits cause the publicly held federal debt to increase.[1] The FY2009 deficit of 10% of GDP, in a year when GDP fell, caused the debt-to-GDP ratio to rise by 12.6 percentage points. The debt has increased from 41% of GDP in 2008 to 73% of GDP in 2012. This was the highest the debt has been relative to GDP since World War II, when it peaked at 109% of GDP.

The current policy debate on the "fiscal cliff"[2] occurring at the end of 2012 has raised the question of whether a deficit of the current magnitude is manageable and what risks it poses to the economy. Since deficit reduction could have a contractionary effect on the economy in the short run at a time when the economy is still fragile[3] restoring fiscal sustainability poses another set of risks that must be balanced against the risks of continuing an unsustainably large deficit. This report will evaluate sustainability issues.

AT WHAT POINT DOES THE PUBLIC DEBT BECOME UNSUSTAINABLE?

Some economists worry that if the public debt keeps rising, it will become unsustainable. By definition, the debt becomes unsustainable when private investors are no longer willing to hold it, at least at normal interest rates. Private investors become unwilling to hold a nation's debt when they become convinced that the government will either default on (in other words, renege on promises to repay) or monetize the debt (in other words, finance it through money creation) in a way that would result in rapidly increasing price inflation that reduces the existing debt's relative value.

Although it is not possible to establish a threshold level at which a country's debt becomes unsustainable, the trend that causes unsustainability is well known: a country cannot continually increase its debt at a rate that exceeds the growth rate of the economy. When it does, it causes debt service to absorb more and more of national income. As private investors observe that the government is unable or unwilling to make policy changes to prevent the debt burden from increasing, they will decide to flee the country's debt before the point where the government is forced to default or monetize. The decision by some investors to flee the debt will make it more onerous for the government to finance the debt, because it will now have to offer higher yields to attract new buyers, and higher yields will result in a larger deficit and more borrowing. This phenomenon is sometimes referred to as a "debt spiral." Thus, unsustainability tends to be triggered rapidly, as no investor wants to be the one still holding the debt when eventual default or hyperinflation occurs. The exact point when investors choose to flee depends on psychological factors that are hard to predict and likely to vary by country.

Because it is the upward trend in debt that leads to unsustainability, investors may accept very large deficits for a few years, as long as they are convinced that in the future the government will reduce the deficit to a sustainable level before it is too late. For example, governments are often able to finance large deficits in wartime—the largest deficits relative to GDP in U.S. history occurred as a result of the Civil War, World War I, and World War II—because investors expect a rapid decline in the deficit once peacetime leads to a rapid decline in military spending.

Investors' willingness to accept large deficits for a time will depend in part on the current level of debt relative to GDP. In that regard, the 16 percentage point reduction in debt to GDP between 1993 and 2001 left the United States in a relatively good starting position to absorb the 30 percentage point increase in debt to GDP that has occurred since 2001. Although the increase in debt in 2012 brings the federal debt as a share of GDP to its highest level since 1950, it will remain at less than three-quarters of its World War II peak.[4]

Are Financial Markets Treating the Debt as Unsustainable?

Standard financial market measures currently do not suggest widespread concern about potential U.S. default. Although investors' views on the sustainability of the deficit cannot be observed directly, they are implicit in Treasury yields. If investors believed that the government would default on its debt or erode its value through inflation, they would demand higher yields to compensate against these risks. Yet Treasury yields have gone down, instead of up, as the deficit has increased. Since the financial crisis, long-term yields have been below 3% for the first time since the 1950s. Besides Treasury yields, another indicator of market fears of default are prices for credit default swaps, which can be thought of as a type of insurance against default.[5] Although the cost of credit default swaps for U.S. Treasuries rose during the recent financial crisis to atypical levels, they still implied a very low probability of default and the rise was much less than in European countries affected by the sovereign debt crisis, discussed below.[6] (They have fallen since.) These data strongly indicate that investors do believe that future deficits will be reduced to sustainable levels.

The ease of financing this year's historically large deficit is partly attributable to unique economic conditions. The United States entered its longest post-war recession in December 2007 (which ended in June 2009), featuring the most severe disruption to financial markets since the Great Depression.[7] September 2008 saw a "flight to quality" by investors who shunned risky assets and sought to hold only the safest assets. Investors perceived Treasury securities to be the safest assets, partly because they are the most liquid (i.e., easily tradeable).

While investors have not shown widespread concern about the sustainability of government borrowing so far, this does not prove that borrowing is on a sustainable path. Investor behavior is compatible with a belief that policy steps will be taken to reduce the deficit to a level that stabilizes debt compared to GDP, but there is no guarantee that the government will take those steps. There is nothing preventing investors from re-evaluating their views at any time, however. As long as federal deficits remain at unsustainable levels, there is the risk—however small—that interest rates could rise quickly as a result of a perceived rise in default risk.[8] Waiting until investor confidence has fallen would require larger policy changes because higher interest rates would cause debt service costs to rise.

Evidence from Abroad

A frequent question is whether one can predict when the United States will reach a "tipping point" where investors become unwilling to finance it. One way to answer that question is to look at whether there is a specific level of public debt that has become problematic for other countries. Different countries have different reputations, so an acceptable debt level is likely to vary from country to country. Because more developing countries have defaulted on their debt in recent decades, advanced economies are generally seen as more able to sustain higher debt levels than developing ones. Thus, in gauging how much higher the U.S. public debt could get before it faces sustainability concerns, it is more useful to compare the United States to other advanced economies.

All of the advanced countries that have experienced fiscal and financial crises (Greece, Iceland, Ireland, Italy, Portugal, and Spain) in recent years have high government debt levels in 2012. This would appear to offer evidence that high debt levels cause fiscal and financial crises, but for some of these countries, causality ran in the opposite direction—Iceland, Ireland, and Spain all had extremely low government debt levels (much lower than the United States) and were running budget surpluses before the crisis. Those three countries have high government debt levels only as a result of the crisis, notably as a result of declining revenue bases, higher social insurance outlays, and their governments taking on liabilities to shore up the banking system. In other words, looking at high public debt levels before the crisis would not have helped predict that those three countries would experience crises. Italy and Greece had unusually high debt levels before the crisis, supporting the idea that high debt can sometimes lead to crisis.[9] On the other hand, Japan's public debt level was by far the highest among advanced countries in 2007, and its borrowing costs have remained unusually low. [10] Japan's ability to finance debt at this level at low interest rates has been attributed to Japan's high overall rate of national saving, despite its large budget deficits, and its near-zero inflation rates.

A comparison of the United States to other advanced economies reveals that the U.S. debt level was higher than average as a share of GDP in 2007, but there were six countries in the sample with debt levels that were higher still. In 2012, the U.S. debt to GDP ratio was higher than most other countries, but well below the ratio in the highest debt countries. The levels of debt to GDP in the United States and many other countries are higher today than any country in 2007 except Greece and Japan.[11]

The concept of a debt spiral is well illustrated by the experience of the eurozone crisis countries. Before the crisis, none of these European countries paid significantly more than Germany to finance government debt. All except Iceland joined the euro area, and their interest rate differentials with Germany fell significantly after joining. This pattern of interest rates implies that markets perceived them as having little more sovereign risk than Germany until the financial crisis, but significantly more afterward. The experience of these countries demonstrates that a loss of confidence quickly leads to a vicious cycle—investors demand higher yields on government debt to compensate against the perceived higher risk of default, but these higher yields cause the deficit to spike suddenly, thereby undermining a government's ability to continue to service its debt. This dynamic causes a country to swing from stability to crisis relatively quickly. Restoring stability has been difficult, and since 2008 GDP has shrunk for three or more years for most of the countries. Falling GDP exacerbates the budget deficit, and vice versa.

These countries that have required assistance to finance their deficits have some commonalities with the United States—projections of unsustainably large budget deficits under current policy, a large net foreign debt (with the exception of Italy), asset price bubbles that led to large losses in the financial sector, and large subsequent government outlays to cope with financial sector turmoil. On the other hand, several factors differentiate the United States from most of these countries—a reputation of fiscal solvency based on a history of non-default, a large economy, a flexible exchange rate, and a status as the world's "reserve currency" and "safe haven." The fact that Treasury securities are considered the riskless, "safe haven" asset internationally could mean that investors continue financing unsustainable deficits longer than they would for other countries, but it could also mean that if confidence were lost, the shift out of Treasury securities would be greater than in other countries since the original rationale for holding them was no longer valid.

Will Future Budget Deficits Remain at Unsustainable Levels Under Current Policy?

If the budget deficit were to remain near 2009 to 2012 levels, it would be unsustainable because it would cause the national debt to continually rise relative to GDP. But will deficits remain at elevated levels in future years, or return to more normal levels under current policy? In other words, are policy changes needed to return the budget to sustainability?

The deficit has already fallen from 10% to 7% of GDP, and there are reasons to believe that the deficit will continue to fall somewhat without any policy changes in the next few years. The recession caused certain outlays (such as unemployment insurance) to automatically rise and revenues to automatically fall. If business cycle conditions continue to improve, deficits will continue to decline. Furthermore, because of "real bracket creep," the tax system tends to collect modestly more revenue each year without any changes to the tax code.[12]

CBO's projections of current law under the baseline show deficits falling to less than 3% of GDP after 2013. The projections would seem to indicate that the budget deficit is already on a sustainable path under current law. These projections assume four important differences from current policy, however. First, CBO assumes that all tax provisions, including the tax cuts enacted in 2001 and 2003, will be allowed to expire as scheduled.[13] Second, CBO projections of the deficit are based on assumptions that the automatic spending reduction process under the Budget Control Act will proceed as scheduled beginning in January 2013.[14] Third, CBO assumes that the routinely enacted one-year "patches" to adjust the alternative minimum tax (AMT) for inflation will not be extended, and as a result millions more taxpayers will pay the AMT each year.[15] Fourth, the Medicare cuts required in law by the sustainable growth physician payment formula are assumed to be allowed to take place; Congress has enacted legislative overrides to prevent those cuts (popularly known as the "doc fix") each year since 2003.[16] If any of these assumptions were altered, deficits would be much higher, all else equal.

Under its Alternative Fiscal Scenario, CBO modifies the baseline to assume that these four current policies stay in place. This causes the projected deficits to fall no lower than 4.2% of GDP, rising as a share of GDP after 2018. Deficits of this size would cause a persistent increase in the debt as a share of GDP; therefore, policy changes are required to put the projected budget deficit on a sustainable path.[17] For illustrative purposes, CRS estimates that to stabilize debt as a share of GDP at its projected 2012 level would require annual budget deficits no larger than 31/2% of GDP in 2015 and 2016, falling to 23/4% of GDP from 2019 on, based on CBO's projections of GDP growth and interest rates. Were GDP to grow more slowly or interest rates to be higher than projected, the deficit would have to be smaller to be sustainable, and vice versa. Compared with a current policy baseline where discretionary spending grows at the rate of inflation, this would require some combination of spending cuts and tax increases equivalent to roughly $800 billion in 2013, falling to $275 billion in 2015, and rising each year thereafter until it exceeds $900 billion in 2022.[18] Thus, deficits do not fall enough under current policy, as defined in CBO's Alternative Fiscal Scenario, to stabilize the debt.

Moreover, long-term projections of current policy estimate that a large increase in Social Security, Medicare, and Medicaid spending will cause the budget deficit to grow continuously following the retirement of the baby boomers. Although deficit projections show some improvement in the short run, the long-term projection estimates even larger deficits under current policy, assuming health care costs continue to rise more rapidly than output. In the long term, reducing the growth rate of health care costs below the growth rate of the economy would have the largest impact on the budget deficit; however, the effects of health care cost growth on the deficit are very gradual, and play little role in the sustainability of the deficit in the near term.[19]

Because interest rates are currently so low, interest payments have been relatively low in recent years despite large deficits. For example, CBO recorded debt service payments of $187 billion for FY2009, the lowest level in dollar terms since 2005, even though the debt rose by more than $1.7 trillion that year. As discussed below, financing the deficit may become more costly once economic conditions normalize. Even if interest rates return only to average levels in recent years, the cost of debt service will rise significantly. CBO's projections assume a relatively low interest rate paid on government debt over the next 10 years, largely because the starting point for its projections is today's historically low rates. Some commentators have questioned whether this assumption is reasonable given the size of current and projected budget deficits. If investors respond to large deficits by demanding above-average interest rates, the cost of debt service would become large. CBO estimates that if interest rates rose to their average level from 1991 to 2000, the budget deficit would be an average of $100 billion higher per year over the next 10 years. If interest rates rose to their average level from 1981 to 1990, the budget deficit would be an average of $500 billion higher per year over the next 10 years.[20]

Sustainability and Foreign Holders of the Debt

Some economists believe the government's reliance on foreign investors to finance the federal debt makes the United States more vulnerable to sudden shifts in investors' willingness to hold federal debt.[21] Foreigners currently hold $5.3 trillion (more than half) of the total privately held federal debt.[22] Foreigners are perceived as less willing to passively buy and hold federal debt, in part because they bear exchange-rate risk when holding federal debt. If so, their demand for federal debt could be more sensitive to perceptions of sustainability, since default or monetization typically leads to currency devaluation that would reduce the debt's value in foreign currencies. If foreigners were to become less willing to hold federal debt, presumably, significantly higher interest rates would be required for Americans to absorb such large sums. For example, J.P. Morgan estimates that a 20% decline in foreign demand for Treasury securities would raise Treasury yields by 0.5 percentage points.[23] Furthermore, if debt service costs were to rise suddenly, higher debt payments to foreigners would result in a fall in U.S. income, while higher debt payments to Americans would transfer income with no net effect on overall U.S. income.

Is foreign unwillingness to hold U.S. debt in the future a serious concern? Perhaps the strongest argument against it is the behavior of investors during the recent financial crisis. Although the crisis first emerged in U.S. subprime mortgage markets, foreigners increased their net purchases of Treasury securities from $155 billion in 2007 to $710 billion in 2008—a trend that continued even after financial conditions deteriorated in September 2008. These circumstances seem like a good test of whether foreigners would be willing to maintain their Treasury holdings in adverse circumstances, and they were.

Nevertheless, in the long run, the sustainability of foreign borrowing falls under the same mathematical rules as the sustainability of government borrowing—the net debt owed to foreigners cannot indefinitely rise faster than GDP, or else an ever-increasing share of national income will be needed to service it. The current account deficit has fallen significantly relative to GDP since 2007, but it remains to be seen whether this change is cyclical or longer lasting. Thus, independent of concerns about the size of the federal debt, the upward trend in the net debt owed to foreigners raises concerns about the long-term sustainability of large-scale borrowing from abroad.[24]

The continued willingness of foreign investors to hold U.S. Treasury securities is further complicated by the role of foreign governments. From the end of 2001 to the second quarter of 2012, foreign official holdings of Treasury securities increased from $0.6 trillion to $3.9 trillion.[25] While it can be reasonably assumed that private investors are purchasing Treasury securities because they are seen as good investments (and would sell them if they no longer were), foreign governments may have other motivations. Countries may have been accumulating official reserves in recent years (1) to prevent their currencies from appreciating against the dollar or against a major trading partner's (or competitor's) currency; (2) because the price of a major export, such as oil, had suddenly risen and the country decided to invest some of its windfall in foreign assets; (3) to guard their currency against a sudden withdrawal of investment from their country during a future downturn; or (4) to rebuild their reserves after a prior defense of their currency drained them away. None of these explanations would imply a permanent desire to continuously accumulate official dollar-denominated assets. Regardless of the motivation for initially purchasing Treasury securities, now that some foreign governments hold large portfolios of federal debt, they have an incentive to maximize their return. Collectively, this would call for governments to cooperate to avoid taking actions, such as large sales of holdings, that destabilize Treasury prices. But individually, any particular government has the incentive to sell its holdings before everyone else if it believes that the debt has become unsustainable; this incentive could hamper collective action.

ECONOMIC EFFECTS OF A "DEBT SPIRAL"

Policymakers are currently faced with a dilemma. Reducing the deficit too quickly could have a contractionary effect on the economy at a time when the economy is still far below full employment. But leaving the deficit at an unsustainable size retains the risk that the budget could at some point enter a debt spiral, in which Treasury yields rose sharply and suddenly. Whether this risk is worth taking depends on two factors—how great the risk is of entering a debt spiral (a risk considered by most to be very small), and how serious the economic effects would be.

Assuming the government were to enter a debt spiral, the economic effects would be expected to be negative and potentially severe. How severe would likely depend on how much spillover there would be to other financial markets. Most economists believe that the 2007-2009 recession was the deepest and longest since the Great Depression because it was accompanied by a financial crisis. Moreover, financial crises seem to leave long-lasting effects after the initial crash— economists Reinhart and Reinhart find that in the decade following a financial crisis the median decline in annual GDP growth is one percentage point and unemployment often does not return to its pre-crisis level.[26]

The direct effect of higher interest rates stemming from greater credit risk would be to reduce the market value of existing federal debt, as investors would be willing to pay a lower price (i.e., demand a higher yield) for Treasury securities to compensate for the greater credit risk. This would cause a negative "wealth effect" for debt holders, and debt holders would be expected to reduce their spending in response, although initially by a much smaller factor than the loss of wealth. Since the publicly held debt is projected to reach $10 trillion by the end of FY2011, the wealth effect could potentially be large. The fact that roughly half of this debt is held by foreigners or the Federal Reserve mitigates the wealth effect on domestic spending. The most potentially damaging wealth effects for the broader economy could come from financial institutions that hold Treasury securities. At the end of third quarter of 2012, commercial banks held over $300 billion of Treasury securities, while insurance companies, GSEs, and broker/dealers held over $400 billion. As demonstrated during the 2008 financial crisis, leveraged financial firms can potentially respond to losses that reduce their capital base by contracting credit by a multiple of the amount of losses, a process known as deleveraging.[27] These "leveraged losses" can lead to a credit crunch that affects the economy as a whole.

The potential severity of the effects on the economy would come from indirect effects that are of a more uncertain nature. For example, money market mutual funds held about $450 billion of Treasury securities at the end of the third quarter of 2012. These funds are typically set up to mimic a bank account, in that account balances are quoted with a stable principal that never rises or falls. In the current low interest rate environment, capital losses on Treasury holdings, particularly for funds that are concentrated in Treasury securities, would not have to be that large to cause a fund to "break the buck," meaning that principal would be reduced.[28] When a money market fund broke the buck in September 2008, it set off a $250 billion run on money market funds that was viewed as a significant factor in the worsening of the financial crisis, and was only brought to an end by a temporary government guarantee of money market funds.[29]

Treasury securities are also widely used as collateral for short-term borrowing in the repurchase agreement ("repo") market. The Treasury Borrowing Advisory Committee estimated that Treasury securities are used as collateral for $4 trillion of borrowing, and that this market is an important source of liquidity for leveraged financial firms, such as investment banks.[30] Were the creditworthiness of Treasury securities to be placed in doubt by a debt spiral, lenders could become less willing to accept them as collateral or reduce the amount they were willing to lend against them. Either way, credit would contract and firms' access to liquidity would be harmed if that borrowing could not be replaced in other markets.

A key issue in determining the effects on the broader economy is whether a spike in Treasury yields spilled over into a spike in private yields on corporate bonds, bank lending rates, and consumer credit. Treasury yields are often considered a benchmark lending rate that other private rates are based on (albeit not on a one-to-one basis), although that does not guarantee that they would continue to be if perceptions of sovereign credit risk changed. If financial markets perceived that higher credit risk for the U.S. government did not alter the credit risk of U.S. corporations or households, then private yields would not necessarily rise with Treasury yields. On the other hand, investors may believe that government credit risk implies significant risk for private corporations, in terms of potential financial instability, exchange rate risk, and an inability of the federal government to provide obligated funds or indirect support (such as the resources necessary to maintain financial stability in the event of systemic risk). If so, private yields would rise with Treasury yields.

A debt spiral could also result in the federal government undertaking a contractionary fiscal policy in the form of higher taxes or lower spending. In the mainstream economic model, the direct effects of such a policy would be to further reduce overall spending in the economy in the short run, although in a debt spiral some believe that it might improve confidence in financial markets that partly or wholly offsets the contractionary effects. This is the rationale for countries such as Greece to undertake austerity measures to restore stability.

An obvious limitation to estimating how serious the economic effects of a debt spiral would be is that the United States has not experienced one in modern times. There are examples of foreign countries that have recently become caught in debt spirals, however, and in those countries the contraction in output and employment has typically been deep. In Iceland, GDP fell 11% peak to trough, and in Greece, GDP has already fallen 18% from its peak and is projected to continue falling. By contrast, GDP fell by 2.6% in the United States in the recent recession, which was the deepest since the Great Depression.[31] It is noteworthy that these economic effects have occurred before default occurred, and in cases where financing from neighbors or international institutions such as the International Monetary Fund has allowed the countries to avoid default altogether. Looking more broadly, an IMF study analyzed 148 sovereign defaults between 1824 and 2004, and found that GDP growth declines on average by 2.6 percentage points in the first year after a default.[32] It also worth noting that, typically, countries have eventually bounced back economically—the negative effects have not been permanent. The IMF study found no statistically significant effects on GDP growth after the first year.

To gauge the likelihood of whether a sudden spike in Treasury yields would spill over to the broader economy, a useful analogy might be the recent financial crisis. While the crisis was complex and multi-faceted, the crisis was set off by the unexpected rise in mortgage default rates that caused a broad and widely held class of securities, AAA-rated mortgage-backed securities, to suddenly plummet in value and lose liquidity. The loss in value and liquidity was caused by a reassessment by investors that a security, previously believed to be very safe, in fact faced significant credit risk. The loss in value of these securities was significant enough that it caused financial markets to doubt the solvency of the firms holding the assets. This caused widespread illiquidity for financial firms, and ultimately, some failed. Before the crisis, most economists and policymakers assumed that monetary policy could be employed to contain any systemic risk event, but that proved not to be the case.

Would a Failure to Raise the Debt Limit Cause a Debt Spiral?

The U.S. Treasury has announced that the statutory debt limit would be reached by the end of 2012 under normal operations. If extraordinary measures are taken, the debt limit would not be reached until early 2013.[33] After that point, there would not be enough revenue available to Treasury to finance the spending obligations that have been authorized by Congress under current policy. This has raised the question of whether a failure to raise the debt limit would lead to a default on federal debt. The debt has come close to the statutory limit before, most recently in 2011, but the limit has always been raised before it has been reached. Some commentators have argued that more than enough revenue will be collected to meet interest payments on the debt, so default can be avoided indefinitely. Treasury has argued that it does not have the authority to prioritize between different types of payments, but must meet obligations on a "first in/first out" basis. If so, a failure to meet interest payments could not be avoided since revenue would be insufficient to prevent a backlog of unpaid obligations.[34] A 1985 Government Accountability Office opinion argued that statute does not prevent Treasury from prioritizing and paying interest first.[35]

Assuming Treasury were able to prioritize, although revenues would be sufficient to meet interest payments at current interest rates, a debt spiral might still be unavoidable. As discussed above, investors will continue financing unsustainably large budget deficits as long as they believe that the government will eventually implement policy measures to reduce them to sustainable levels. Some investors might perceive a failure to raise the debt limit as a signal that the "full faith and credit" of the federal government no longer stood behind its obligations, even if the government continued to meet interest payments. This could occur for two reasons. First, if unable to borrow, it would be unlikely that the government would be able to meet all other legal obligations, such as contractual payments to private vendors. Debt holders might decide that if the federal government is unwilling to meet other legal obligations, they may eventually be treated similarly, and flee the debt to avoid that fate. Second, debt holders might decide that a scenario where popular federal programs went unfunded so that interest payments were met would be politically unsustainable, even if it were technically sustainable. Debt holders might conclude that political pressure would eventually cause policymakers to redirect revenues from interest payments toward popular programs, even if they did not. Debt holders might conclude that an unwillingness to raise the debt limit was a sign that policymakers had reached an impasse on fiscal issues that would prevent deficit reduction. (Debt holders might also reach the opposite conclusion—that a failure to raise the debt limit signaled that deficit reduction was more likely in the future.) If debt holders came to doubt the government's future willingness to make interest payments, interest rates would rise. If they rose high enough, revenues (which fluctuate significantly from month to month) would no longer be sufficient to continually meet interest payments even under prioritization.[36]

As discussed above, a debt spiral would be expected to begin before a default, at the point when investors deemed the status quo untenable. If a failure to raise the debt limit led to a debt spiral, the economic effects would be expected to be as described above (see "Economic Effects of a "Debt Spiral").

Would a Ratings Downgrade Cause a Debt Spiral?

On August 5, 2011, Standard & Poor's, a major ratings agency, downgraded U.S. federal debt from AAA to AA+ to

> reflect our opinion that the fiscal consolidation plan that Congress and the Administration recently agreed to falls short of what, in our view, would be necessary to stabilize the government's medium-term debt dynamics. More broadly, the downgrade reflects our view that the effectiveness, stability, and predictability of American policymaking and political institutions have weakened at a time of ongoing fiscal and economic challenges to a degree more than we envisioned when we assigned a negative outlook to the rating on April 18, 2011.[37]

To date, other rating agencies have not downgraded U.S. debt, although Moody's and Fitch changed their ratings outlook to negative in 2011.[38]

If the federal government debt were downgraded again, would that set in motion a debt spiral that could result in significantly higher interest rates and a potential default? Based on market reaction to the 2011 downgrade, the answer would appear to be no. Counterintuitively, Treasury yields fell in the week after the downgrade, and have remained lower since. It appears that Treasury yields fell following the 2011 downgrade because they are desirable to many investors because they are considered to be a "safe haven" asset, and play a central role in world financial markets because of their perceived riskless status, although one might have predicted a downgrade would undermine the "safe haven" status of Treasury securities.

Since the last downgrade had the opposite effect on interest rates that many economists would have predicted, it is difficult to say whether the same pattern would occur in the event of a future downgrade. The answer would depend, in part, on how much the debt was ultimately downgraded. A one-step downgrade would leave U.S. debt several steps above "junk" status, and above many of its peers. A one-step downgrade in a U.S. private or municipal security is not typically a crisis-triggering event; issuers of such securities merely pay a "risk premium" in terms of higher yields than higher-rated peers or relative to what the issuer would have paid had a downgrade not occurred.[39] Many foreign governments are able to issue debt at manageable interest rates, albeit generally higher than the United States, despite a lower credit rating. Japanese government debt, for example, has a lower credit rating than the United States, yet its yields have been consistently lower than U.S. government debt.[40]

On the other hand, as discussed above, as long as the federal budget is on an unsustainable path, investor sentiment could deteriorate at any time. Future downgrades could alter the safe haven role of Treasury securities, although the last downgrade did not. It is hypothetically possible that a ratings downgrade could trigger a sudden deterioration in investor sentiment, similar to how the ratings downgrade of AAA mortgage-backed securities coincided with a fall in their value in 2007-2008. If a downgrade resulted in a debt spiral, the economic effects would be expected to be similar to those described above (see "Economic Effects of a "Debt Spiral").

The impact on the broader economy will depend in part on how the downgrade affects broader financial markets. It does not necessarily follow that a lower credit rating for the federal government would automatically lead to broad rating downgrades for U.S. companies, but in 2011 Standard & Poor's downgraded the debt of several government sponsored enterprises and U.S. insurers from AAA to AA+ as a result of the federal debt downgrade.[41]

Another factor to consider is that, historically, rating downgrades sometimes lag rather than lead market events.[42] This section has implicitly assumed that a downgrade would occur in a scenario of normal financial conditions, similar to the present. Instead, a ratings downgrade could be triggered by some financial market disturbance. In other words, federal debt might not be downgraded until after Treasury yields or other measures of credit risk were already rising. Arguably, this pattern has occurred for the euro debt crisis countries.

Is a Large But Manageable Deficit Harmful to the Economy?

Assuming that the government is able to continue to finance the deficit smoothly, do large deficits have any effect on the economy? When the economy is at full employment (meaning practically all labor and capital resources are in use), government budget deficits "crowd out," or compete with, private investment spending in the standard macroeconomic model. Setting aside foreign capital flows for the moment, borrowing can only be financed through saving, and government borrowing competes with business borrowing for the same pool of national saving. By increasing the demands on that pool of national saving, government borrowing pushes up the cost of all borrowing through higher interest rates, causing businesses to finance less capital spending than they otherwise would.[43] Business borrowing finances capital spending on plant and equipment, and lower capital spending results in lower potential gross domestic product, and hence lower future national income, than would otherwise occur.

In the current context, the economy is not at or near full employment. In this context, government deficits are unlikely to significantly crowd out private business borrowing. On the contrary, business investment was contracting until the fourth quarter of 2009 and has remained low as a share of GDP since, either because investment demand declined or businesses are credit constrained. This greatly reduced the potential for large government deficits to crowd out private investment spending. As discussed above, low interest rates support the view that the deficit is currently causing little crowding out to occur. (Of course, this could change if investor concern about sustainability pushed up interest rates.) In this case, the decline in aggregate spending caused by falling investment spending can be offset, at least in part, by the rise in (deficit-financed) government spending, which directly increases GDP, and (deficit-financed) tax cuts, which directly increase after-tax income. Most economic forecasters projected that the rise in the budget deficit, on balance, increased GDP over the last few years, despite a possible crowding out effect. Indeed, it is the increase in the deficit that is the primary reason that the stimulus act (P.L. 111-5) was projected to stimulate the economy in standard macroeconomic models.[44]

With international capital mobility, borrowing can also be financed by foreign saving. In the standard macroeconomic model with perfect capital mobility, the boost in aggregate spending from the stimulus would cause the trade deficit to rise as foreign capital is attracted to higher domestic interest rates. The availability of foreign credit would avoid the crowding out of domestic capital investment. But the boost to aggregate spending from the budget deficit would be negated (or "crowded out") by the higher trade deficit. The United States relies heavily on foreign borrowing, and this is another reason that large budget deficits could be less effective at stimulating the economy. The lack of perfect capital mobility, and the large output gap at present, in the United States means that a larger trade deficit is unlikely to completely negate the stimulus as theory would suggest, but it is likely to make it less effective at boosting aggregate spending. Since the recession began, the trade deficit has fallen substantially, so a problem of crowding out from the trade deficit is not apparent at this time. It should also be noted that if capital spending is financed by foreigners, the income generated by that capital will accrue to foreigners instead of to Americans.

As the economy returns to full employment, large budget deficits will no longer stimulate aggregate spending.[45] At that point, crowding out will become a more serious concern if the budget deficit is not reduced. By accounting identity, domestic investment must equal national saving plus net borrowing from abroad.[46] In the years before the crisis (2000 to 2007), domestic investment averaged about 20% of GDP, as seen in *Table 1.* Because national saving averaged about 15% of GDP, three-quarters of this investment was financed by national saving and one-quarter was financed by borrowing from abroad. The federal budget deficit modestly reduced national saving during most of that period.[47] In 2008, national saving fell to 12.6% of GDP, in part because the budget deficit rose to 3.2% of GDP. Despite the fall in national saving that year, net borrowing from abroad remained relatively steady because investment spending fell to 17.5% of GDP.

Table 1. Saving, Investment, and the Federal Budget Deficit, 2000-2011
(percentage of GDP)

	2000-2007	2008	2009-2011
Gross Domestic Investment	20.3	18.0	15.2
Gross National Saving	15.4	12.4	11.8
Net Borrowing from Abroad	4.9	4.6	3.0
Federal Budget Deficit[a]	-1.3	-3.2	-9.3

Source: CRS calculations; Congressional Budget Office.

Notes: Gross domestic investment is the sum of private and government investment. Gross national saving is the sum of business, household, and government saving.

[a] Fiscal Year, as measured by federal budget conventions.

The budget deficit averaged 9.3% of GDP from FY2009 to FY2011, more than half the size of total private saving, which is the sum of household and business saving. Although investment was low in 2009-2011 because of the recession and subsequent sluggish recovery, it can be expected to rebound when the economy recovers. At that point, even if the deficit were to fall by half as a share of GDP, either private saving would need to rise significantly above its average over the past 10 years or net borrowing from abroad would have to be significantly higher than the 2000 to 2007 average, which was already at a historical high. Private saving has risen from a range of 14% to 16% of GDP from 2000 to 2007 to an average of 18.9% of GDP in 2009 to 2011, some of which may prove lasting, but many economists question whether it would continue to rise enough to offset the rise in the budget deficit. In other words, even before the rise in the budget deficit, the combination of low rates of national saving and high rates of borrowing from abroad to finance domestic investment spending was unsustainable in the long run. If the budget deficit remains at elevated rates, national saving will be even lower, requiring either lower rates of domestic investment (that would reduce GDP from what it otherwise would have been) or higher rates of borrowing from abroad.

The willingness of private foreign investors to buy U.S. assets in the future will depend not only on the desirability of U.S. investment opportunities, but also on investment opportunities abroad. Here too, future trends may point to a shift away from U.S. assets. Even if foreign investors were unconcerned about the sustainability of U.S. debt, foreign countries may find more internal demand for their saving as the world economy recovers. U.S. public debt will also be competing to attract funds with a large increase in borrowing by foreign governments. The IMF projects that public debt in the advanced economies will rise from 80% of GDP in 2008 to 110% of GDP in 2012.[48] As noted above, many U.S. assets have been bought by foreign governments in the past decade, which may have accumulated U.S. assets for political reasons that cease in the future.

Will Large Deficits Lead to High Inflation?

Another concern that has been raised is that large deficits will lead to high inflation. Inflation is related to changes in the money supply; the Federal Reserve controls the money supply independently of the Treasury and its financing needs. Large deficits would lead to higher inflation if the Fed finances unfunded government operations by increasing the money supply. Under current law, this is prevented by Section 14 of the Federal Reserve Act, which forbids the Federal Reserve from purchasing debt directly from the Treasury, and Section 2A, which mandates that the Fed keep inflation low, among other goals.[49] In a well-known article, economists Thomas Sargent and Neil Wallace pointed out some "unpleasant arithmetic," however.[50] They observed that in order to avoid the economic effects of government default, a central bank might ultimately be forced to monetize the debt if private investors became unwilling to finance it and the government refuses to raise taxes or cut spending. Investors may perceive this future outcome and raise their inflationary expectations today. If investors anticipate that the debt will be monetized, they will require higher interest rates to finance it in the meantime, so inflation will ultimately be higher than if the deficit had been monetized from the outset. In that example, future inflation is a function of fiscal decisions as well as monetary decisions taken today. To date, there is no evidence that inflation expectations have risen significantly.

End Notes

[1] References in this report to the national debt refer to the publicly held federal debt unless otherwise noted because this is the debt that is financed in private capital markets and affects the economy. The gross federal debt, which was 104% of GDP in 2012, is the sum of the publicly held debt and intra-governmental debt that arises from surpluses in government trust funds. Changes in intra-governmental debt are unrelated to the budget deficit.

[2] For more information, see CRS Report R42654, Major Fiscal Issues Before Congress in FY2013, coordinated by Mindy R. Levit.

[3] For more information, see CRS Report R42700, The "Fiscal Cliff": Macroeconomic Consequences of Tax Increases and Spending Cuts, by Jane G. Gravelle.

[4] For more information, see CRS Report RL34712, The Federal Debt: An Analysis of Movements from World War II to the Present, by Mindy R. Levit.

[5] For more information on credit default swaps, see CRS Report RS22932, Credit Default Swaps: Frequently Asked Questions, by Edward V. Murphy and Rena S. Miller.

[6] CMA, Global Sovereign Credit Risk Report, Q1, 2011, http://www.cmavision.com/images/uploads/docs/CMA_Global_Sovereign_Debt_Credit_Risk_Report_Q1_2011.pdf.

[7] See CRS Report R40198, The 2007-2009 Recession: Similarities to and Differences from the Past, by Marc Labonte.

[8] This argument is made, for example, in Chairman Ben Bernanke, "Fiscal Sustainability," Speech, Washington, DC, June 14, 2011, available at http://www.federalreserve.gov/newsevents/speech/bernanke20110614a.htm.

[9] While Italy had a long history of budget deficits, it is notable that its deficit was smaller than average and much smaller than the United States since 2007.

[10] Based on general government gross debt from the IMF, World Economic Outlook, October 2012. Using general government net debt (which nets out certain government assets), the same

pattern is present, although by that measure Japan's debt level was lower than Greece's and Italy's in 2007.

[11] Based on general government gross debt from the IMF, World Economic Outlook, October 2012. Using general government net debt (which nets out certain government assets), the U.S. debt level in 2012 is higher than all countries in 2007 except Greece and Italy.

[12] "Real bracket creep" refers to as incomes rise over time, more income is subject to tax.

[13] For more information, see CRS Report R42485, An Overview of Tax Provisions Expiring in 2012, by Margot L. Crandall-Hollick.

[14] For more information, see CRS Report R41965, The Budget Control Act of 2011, by Bill Heniff Jr., Elizabeth Rybicki, and Shannon M. Mahan.

[15] For more information, see CRS Report RL30149, The Alternative Minimum Tax for Individuals, by Steven Maguire.

[16] For more information, see CRS Report R40907, Medicare Physician Payment Updates and the Sustainable Growth Rate (SGR) System, by Jim Hahn and Janemarie Mulvey.

[17] Budget projections are subject to high margins of error, even over relatively short periods of time. Thus, the actual deficit in future years could turn out to be larger or smaller than CBO's projection, requiring larger or smaller policy changes, respectively, to place the debt on a sustainable path.

[18] CRS estimates from CRS Report R41778, Reducing the Budget Deficit: Policy Issues, by Marc Labonte.

[19] See CRS Report RL32747, The Economic Implications of the Long-Term Federal Budget Outlook, by Marc Labonte.

[20] Congressional Budget Office, Letter to Honorable Paul Ryan, Feb 24, 2011, Table 2.

[21] As an example, J.P. Morgan notes that foreign holdings of GSE debt fell by 40% after they were taken into federal conservatorship following financial problems although the federal government ensured that their debt continued to be paid in full. See " J.P. Morgan, "The Domino Effect of a U.S. Treasury Technical Default," U.S. Fixed Income Strategy, April 19, 2011. See also, Kenneth Rogoff, "Foreign Holdings of U.S. Debt: Is Our Economy Vulnerable?", Testimony before the Committee on the Budget, U.S. House of Representatives, June 26, 2007; Brad Setser, U.S. External Debt and Power, Brookings Institute, working paper, 2008.

[22] Federal Reserve, Flow of Funds, Table L.209. Privately held debt omits debt held by government trust funds and the Federal Reserve. It includes debt held by state and local governments.

[23] J.P. Morgan, "The Domino Effect of a U.S. Treasury Technical Default," U.S. Fixed Income Strategy, April 19, 2011, http://www.jpmorgan.com/cm/Satellite?blobcol= urldata&blob header=application%2Fpdf&blobkey=id& blobtable=MungoBlobs&blobwhere=1158634891053&ssbinary=true.

[24] For more information, see CRS Report RL33186, Is the U.S. Current Account Deficit Sustainable?, by Marc Labonte.

[25] For more information, see CRS Report RS21951, Financing the U.S. Trade Deficit: Role of Foreign Governments, by Marc Labonte.

[26] Carmen Reinhart and Vincent Reinhart, "After the Fall," National Bureau of Economic Research, Working Paper 16334, September 2010. See also International Monetary Fund, World Economic Outlook, Oct. 2009, Ch. 4.

[27] Financial firms can respond to losses that deplete their capital by raising new capital to replenish it or reducing the size of their overall balance sheet to return to previous leverage ratios. In the 2008 financial crisis, the difficulty that firms had in raising new capital led many to deleverage in response to losses.

[28] The effect of interest rate changes on the value of Treasury securities held by money market funds is reduced by the fact that these funds are limited to securities with short-term maturities. Nevertheless, J.P. Morgan estimates that a sudden increase in yields of 1.5 to 1.75 percentage point or larger would cause some money market mutual funds to "break the buck." J.P. Morgan, "The Domino Effect of a U.S. Treasury Technical Default," U.S. Fixed Income Strategy, April 19, 2011, http://www.jpmorgan.com/cm/Satellite?blobcol=urldata&blob header=application%2Fpdf& blobkey=id&blobtable=MungoBlobs&blobwhere=1158634891053&ssbinary=true. Unless Treasury defaulted, any capital losses would be unrealized ("mark-to-market" losses). However, although money market funds are allowed to value their holdings at historical cost, they must take prompt action if the mark-tomarket cost deviates from the historical cost by more than 0.005%. See BlackRock, "The New Regulatory Regime for Money Market Funds," Viewpoint, Jan. 2011, https://www2.blackrock.com/webcore/litService/search/ get Document.seam?contentId=1111128717&Source=SEARCH&Venue=PUB_INS.

[29] Figure cited in Fed Chairman Ben Bernanke, "Financial Reform to Address Systemic Risk," speech at the Council on Foreign Relations, March 10, 2009, http://www.federal reserve.gov/newsevents/speech/bernanke20090310a.htm. For more information, see CRS Report R41073, Government Interventions in Response to Financial Turmoil, by Baird Webel and Marc Labonte.

[30] Matthew Zames, Treasury Borrowing Advisory Committee, Letter to the Honorable Timothy Geithner, April 25, 2011, http://www.sifma.org/issues/item.aspx?id=25013.

[31] CRS calculations using annual data from International Monetary Fund. These calculations may underestimate the peak to trough decline in GDP because they use annual data.

[32] Eduardo Borensztein and Ugo Panizza, "The Costs of Sovereign Default," International Monetary Fund, Working Paper 08/238, October 2008. Because default could cause recession or recession could cause default, the authors use statistical tests to verify that the negative effects on GDP growth are caused by the default, although they find a smaller effect on GDP when using these tests.

[33] U.S. Treasury, Quarterly Refunding Statement, November 2012, http://www.treasury.gov/ press-center/press-releases/ Pages/tg1753.aspx.

[34] FitchRatings, a major rating agency, announced that even short delays (so-called "technical default") in payment to bondholders could trigger a ratings downgrade, and "though such an event (such as a short-lived Treasury bill default) might not permanently impair the capacity of the U.S. government to service its obligations, it is unlikely that its 'AAA' status would be retained in the short to medium term." FitchRatings, "Thinking the Unthinkable – What if the Debt Ceiling Was Not Increased and the U.S. Defaulted?," Comment, June 8, 2011.

[35] These issues are analyzed in greater detail in CRS Report R41633, Reaching the Debt Limit: Background and Potential Effects on Government Operations, coordinated by Mindy R. Levit.

[36] See Chairman Ben Bernanke, "Fiscal Sustainability," Speech, Washington, DC, June 14, 2011.

[37] Standard & Poor's, United States of America Long-Term Rating Lowered to 'AA+' on Political Risks and Rising Debt Burden, August 5, 2011.

[38] Moody's Investors Service, Moody's Confirms U.S. Aaa Rating, Assigns Negative Outlook, Aug. 2, 2011. Drew Fitzgerald, "Fitch Lowers Outlook on U.S. Sovereign-Debt Rating to Negative," Dow Jones Newswires, November 28, 2011.

[39] J.P. Morgan estimates a one notch downgrade in the federal government's credit rating would increase Treasury yields by one percentage point. J.P. Morgan, "The Domino Effect of a U.S. Treasury Technical Default," U.S. Fixed Income Strategy, April 19, 2011,

http://www.jpmorgan.com/cm/Satellite?blobcol=urldata&blobheader=application%2Fpdf&blobkey=id&blobtable=MungoBlobs&blobwhere=1158634891053&ssbinary=true.

[40] Stanley White and Rie Ishiguro, "Fitch Cuts Japan Credit Rating Outlook to Negative," Reuters, May 27, 2011.

[41] Standard & Poor's, "Ratings on Select GREs And FDIC- and NCUA-Guaranteed Debt Lowered After Sovereign Downgrade," August 8, 2011; Standard & Poor's, "Rating Actions Taken On 10 U.S.-Based Insurance Groups Following Sovereign Downgrade," August 8, 2011.

[42] See Gordon Delianedis and Robert Geske, "Credit Risk and Risk Neutral Default Probabilities," The Anderson School at UCLA working paper, February 2003; Carmen Reinhart, "Credit Ratings, Default, and Financial Crises," World Bank Economic Review, vol. 16, no. 2, 2002, pp. 151-170.

[43] In the case of current budget deficits, some government borrowing is being used to purchase assets from the financial sector, notably preferred stock. Borrowing to buy assets would not be expected to have the same crowding out effect as borrowing to buy goods and services. Asset purchases are not the primary cause of the current budget deficit, however.

[44] See, for example, Congressional Budget Office, Estimated Impact of the American Reinvestment and Recovery Act on Employment and Economic Output, May 2011.

[45] An economy near full employment does not have much slack that can be spurred into use by stimulus. Further, in the standard model, it is the increase in the deficit that stimulates spending—were the level of the deficit to be held steady, the economy would receive no further stimulus in future years.

[46] National saving is comprised of business saving, household saving, and government saving. Most national saving in the 2000s came from business saving; household saving averaged close to zero. When the government budget is in deficit, government saving is negative.

[47] In 2000 and 2001, the federal government ran a budget surplus that increased national saving. From 2002 to 2007, the government ran a deficit that reduced national saving. The deficit was more than 2% of GDP from 2003 to 2005, and less than 2% of GDP in the other years.

[48] International Monetary Fund, World Economic Outlook database, October 2012.

[49] While the law forbids the Fed to directly finance the deficit, it can indirectly reduce the government's financing costs by purchasing Treasury securities on the secondary market. While the Treasury must pay the Fed interest on the Treasury securities it holds, the Fed remits its profits to the Treasury. The Fed has purchased Treasury securities on the secondary market since 2009 in order to stimulate the economy, but to date inflation has remained low.

[50] Thomas Sargent and Neil Wallace, "Some Unpleasant Monetarist Arithmetic," Federal Reserve Bank of Minneapolis, Quarterly Review, Fall 1981.

In: Federal Deficits and Debt
Editor: Jamie Malone

ISBN: 978-1-53610-268-0

Chapter 4

OVERVIEW OF THE FEDERAL DEBT*

D. Andrew Austin

SUMMARY

The size of current and projected federal deficits and the accumulation of federal debt are central to current congressional deliberations regarding fiscal reforms. This report provides a broad overview of the federal debt, annual budget deficits, and debt service costs. Federal debt is the accumulated sum of unrepaid borrowing by the federal government over time. The total federal debt consists of *debt held by the public* and *intragovernmental* debt. Debt owed to the public represents borrowing from entities other than the federal government, and includes borrowing from state and local governments, foreign governments and investors, the Federal Reserve System, and foreign central banks, as well as private investors in the United States.

Intragovernmental debt consists of debt liabilities owed by one part of the federal government to another, which are mostly held in trust funds. The Social Security Old Age and Survivors' Insurance (OASI) account is the federal trust fund with the largest holdings of Treasury securities. The largest 20 trust funds account for about 98% of intragovernmental debt. The Social Security trust funds were designed to provide financial resources to pay future benefits. The federal government, however, must raise revenues, cut spending, or borrow in order to obtain funds that will allow the U.S. Treasury to redeem the trust fund securities in the future.

---

* This is an edited, reformatted and augmented version of a Congressional Research Service publication, CRS Report for Congress R41815, from www.crs.gov, dated May 11, 2011.

Nearly all federal debt is subject to a statutory limit. On April 29, 2011, debt subject to limit was $14,236 billion, about $58 billion below the current statutory debt limit of $14,294 billion. The U.S. Treasury projects federal debt will reach its statutory limit before May 16, 2011, although extraordinary measures could extend Treasury's borrowing capacity until about August 2, 2011.

The U.S. Treasury uses various debt instruments to manage its cash and debt, so that funds are available to fund outlays and costs of carrying federal debt are minimized. Even when the federal budget is in balance, Treasury would still have to issue some debt to balance out seasonal fluctuations in revenues and outlays.

For most of American history, federal debt was closely linked to war finance. In recent decades, the growing costs of federally financed health care and other entitlement spending have played an important role in the government's fiscal situation. Higher spending on defense and other security costs, as well as tax cuts and other tax policy decisions, have also influenced the size of federal deficits and the accumulation of debt.

Interest rates on federal debt have fallen to extremely low levels due to the effects of the 2007- 2008 financial crises and subsequent recession. As the economy continues to recover interest rates will likely rise. Federal debt levels, according to projections, will continue to increase in coming years. Thus, net interest costs are projected to rise rapidly. According to April 2011 CBO baseline projections, net interest costs will rise from $213 billion in FY2011 to $534 billion in FY2016.

A growing proportion of the federal debt is held by foreign investors and governments as capital markets have become more international. Some countries, especially in East Asia, have had very high savings rates that have financed significant accumulations of federal debt.

Federal debt is a backward-looking reflection of the government's fiscal condition. Some forward-looking measures of the federal debt may more accurately reflect the federal government's fiscal condition and its ability to face future budgetary challenges. This report will be updated as events warrant.

INTRODUCTION

The size of current and projected federal deficits and the accumulation of federal debt are central to current congressional deliberations regarding fiscal reforms. This report provides a broad overview of the federal debt, annual budget deficits, debt service costs, and related issues. Citations to other CRS reports that provide more detail on these topics are included.[1]

This report describes the structure of the federal debt, which is divided between debt held by the public (i.e., held by entities other than the federal government) and intragovernmental debt. Most debt held by the public is marketable, while all but a tiny portion of intragovernmental debt is nonmarketable and held in federal trust funds. The workings of federal trust funds and the federal debt limit are then briefly described.

While the federal debt is the accumulation of annual deficits, reconciling a deficit with the yearover-year increase in federal debt requires certain technical adjustments (discussed below). The report then discusses the relationship between deficits and the federal debt, and the history of the debt in recent decades.

A following section discusses elements of federal debt management. The U.S. Treasury aims to maintain a mix of maturities among securities making up the federal debt that minimize borrowing costs and risks associated with changing market conditions. Interest yields on fixed income securities, such as Treasury bills, notes, and bonds, depend on their maturity (i.e., how long until a security is redeemed).

Finally, the report examines ownership of publicly held debt, both in terms of the nationality and the type of investor (insurers, mutual funds, etc.).

STRUCTURE OF THE FEDERAL DEBT

Federal debt is the accumulated sum of unrepaid borrowing by the federal government over time.

The total federal debt consists of *debt held by the public* and *intragovernmental* debt. Debt owed to the public represents borrowing from entities other than the federal government, and includes borrowing from state and local governments, foreign governments and investors, the Federal Reserve System, foreign central banks, as well as private investors in the United States. Intragovernmental debt consists of debt liabilities owed by one part of the federal government to another, which are mostly held in trust funds. Federal debt at the end of calendar 2010, split by intragovernmental and publicly held components, is shown in Figure 1.

Debt Held by the Public

Table 1 provides a breakdown of publicly held debt.[2] As of December 31, 2010, total federal debt outstanding was $14,025 billion, debt held by the public was $9,390 billion, and intragovernmental debt was $4,613 billion. The bulk of debt held by the public is in the form of marketable securities that can be freely traded in capital markets. U.S. savings bonds are an example of nonmarketable federal debt held by the public. Nearly all intragovernmental debt is nonmarketable.

Table 2 shows components of intragovernmental debt for the end of calendar years 2009 and 2010. Large federal deficits in recent years have translated into large increases in debt held by the public. This increase is reflected across all types of marketable debt instruments (i.e., bills, notes, bonds, and TIPS), although in calendar year 2010 the largest increase was in notes. The U.S. Treasury chooses a mixture of various debt instruments to manage its cash and debt so that funds are available to fund outlays and costs of carrying federal debt are minimized. Even when the federal budget is in balance, Treasury must still issue some debt to balance out seasonal fluctuations in revenues and outlays.

The marketable portion of the debt held by the public consists of U.S. Treasury securities that are generally sold at scheduled auctions.[3] Treasury securities are available in various maturities. Shorter-maturity Treasury securities normally have lower yields and provide more flexibility in cash management. Long maturity bonds, while normally requiring higher interest rates, can protect borrowers, such as the federal government, against the risk of interest rate increases in the medium and long term.

The largest components of the nonmarketable portion of debt held by the public are the State and Local Government Series (SLGS) and U.S. Savings Bonds and other Savings Securities.[4] SLGSs are customized securities available for state and local governments to hold proceeds of bond sales. SLGSs were designed to limit state and local governments' ability to deposit proceeds of tax-exempt bond issues, which generally carry interest rates below non-exempt securities, into bank accounts earning higher interest rates. This could allow state and local governments to earn arbitrage profits at the expense of federal taxpayers.[5] U.S. Savings Bonds were widely promoted to fund World War II, but now account for a small portion of federal debt.

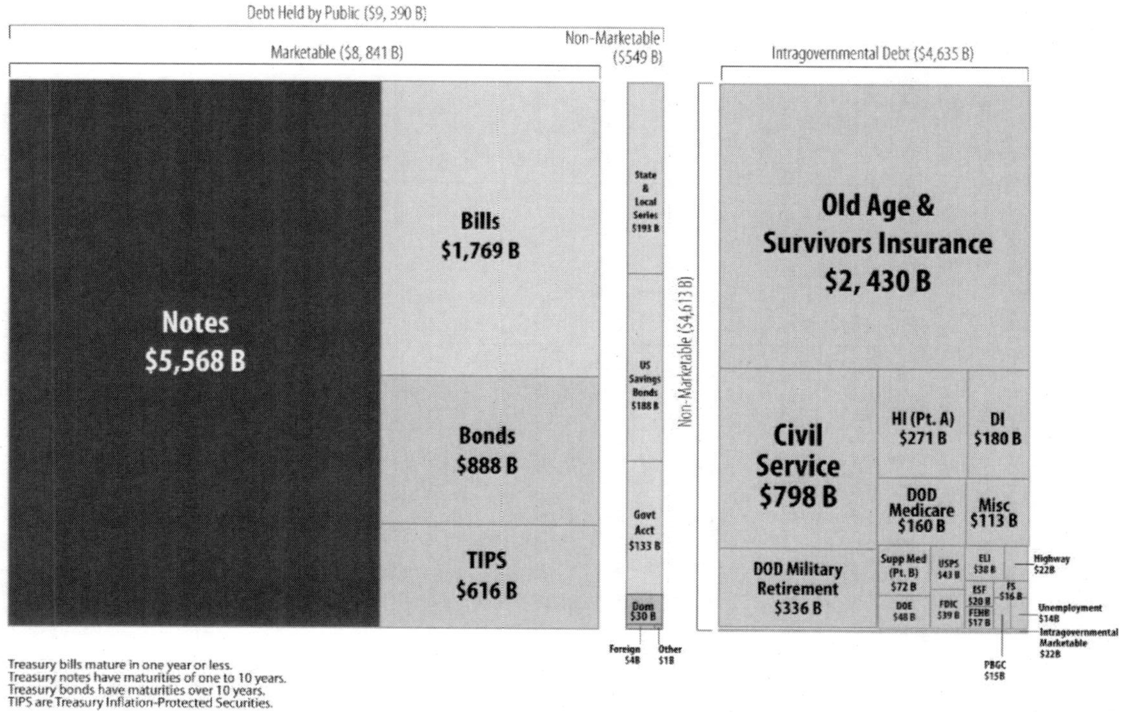

Source: CRS analysis of U.S. Treasury data. Notes: Total federal debt outstanding at the end of December 31, 2010, was $14,025 billion. See text and Tables 1 and 2.

Figure 1. Structure of Federal Debt; $Billions, end of calendar year 2010.

The Government Account within the nonmarketable portion of debt held by the public mostly comprises funds belonging to the Thrift Savings Plan (TSP), a defined contribution plan for federal employees. The Government Account also includes various escrow, claims, and settlement funds.

Table 1. Federal Debt Held by the Public
$Billions

	End of 2009	End of 2010
Marketable		
Bills maturity ≤ 1 year	1,788	1,769
Notes maturity : 1 to 10 years	4,179	5,568
Bonds maturity > 10 years	715	888
TIPS Treasury Inflation Protected Securities	568	616
Subtotal	7,250	8,841
Nonmarketable		
State & Local Series	214	193
U.S. Savings Bonds	191	188
Government Account	120	133
Domestic	30	30
Foreign	4	4
Other	1	1
	End of 2009	End of 2010
Subtotal	561	549
Total Debt Held by Public	7,811	9,390

Source: U.S. Treasury, *Treasury Bulletin*, December 2010, and *Monthly Statement of the Public Debt*, January 2011.

Table 2. Federal Intragovernmental Debt
$Billions, end of calendar years 2009 and 2010

Fund Name	Abbreviation	2009	2010
Federal Old-Age & Survivors Insurance Trust Fund (Social Security)	OASI	2318.8	2429.5
Federal Disability Insurance Trust Fund (Social Security)	DI	199.8	180.0
Hospital Insurance Trust Fund (Medicare)	HI (Pt. A)	304.6	271.4

Fund Name	Abbreviation	2009	2010
Supplementary Medical Insurance Trust Fund (Medicare)	Supp Med (Pt. B)	75.9	71.7
Civil Service Retirement & Disability Fund (OPM)	Civil Service	750.2	777.8
Fund Name	Abbreviation	2009	2010
Military Retirement Fund (Defense)	DoD Mil Ret	295.8	335.9
Medicare Eligible Retiree Fund (Defense)	DoD Medicare	144.6	160.0
Nuclear Waste Disposal Fund (Energy)	DOE	45.4	47.8
Postal Service Retiree Health Benefits Fund	USPS	35.9	42.9
Deposit Insurance Fund	FDIC	59.5	39.4
Employees' Life Insurance Fund (OPM)	ELI	36.7	38.2
Highway Trust Fund	Highway	7.6	22.3
Exchange Stabilization Fund (Treasury)	ESF	19.2	20.4
Employees' Health Benefits Fund (OPM)	FEHB	15.5	16.8
Foreign Service Retirement & Disability Fund	FS	15.6	16.1
Pension Benefit Guaranty Corporation	PBGC	13.9	14.5
Unemployment Trust Fund	Unemployment	16.2	14.3
Miscellaneous	Misc	122.0	113.3
Subtotal, Intragovernmental Government		4477.2	4612.4
Hope Bonds		0.5	0.5
Subtotal, Intragovernmental Nonmarketable		4477.7	4612.9
Treasury Securities		10.7	11.6
Federal Financing Bank		11.9	10.2
Subtotal, Intragovernmental Marketable		22.6	21.8
Total, Intragovernmental		4500.3	4634.7

Source: U.S. Treasury, *Monthly Treasury Statement* and *Monthly Statement of Public Debt*, December 31, 2009 and 2010, available at http://www.fms.treas.gov/mts/backissues.html and http://www.treasurydirect.gov/govt/reports/ pd/mspd/mspd.htm respectively.

Notes: Abbreviation column shows labels for boxes in Figure 1. See source for other notes.

Intragovernmental Debt[6]

Nearly all intragovernmental debt is held by trust funds and other accounts held at the U.S. Treasury on behalf of various government programs.[7] These funds receive interest payments from the U.S. Treasury, generally in the form of additional Treasury securities. For the largest trust funds, these interest payments occur twice a year, once at the end of June, and again at the end of December. The Social Security Old Age and Survivors' Insurance (OASI) account is the federal trust fund with the largest holdings of Treasury securities. The largest 20 trust funds account for about 98% of intragovernmental debt.[8]

Nearly all intragovernmental debt is nonmarketable. Debt held by the Federal Financing Bank (FFB), which is limited to $15 billion, is nonmarketable and is not generally subject to the debt limit. The Federal Financing Bank was created to increase the efficiency of the federal government's budgetary and financial operations.

How Federal Trust Funds Work

For illustrative purposes, the interactions between the Social Security trust funds, the general fund, and the debt limit are described here. The Old Age and Survivors' Insurance (OASI) and the Disability Insurance (DI) trust funds are the two Social Security trust funds. Other government trust funds may interact with revenue streams and the general funds in somewhat different ways.

Social Security collects revenues from payroll taxes paid by workers and employers, as well as federal income taxes paid by some beneficiaries on a portion of their benefits. In addition, Social Security earns interest income from trust fund investments, which the U.S. Treasury credits to the trust funds in the form of additional government securities.

By law, the Social Security trust funds must be invested in interest-bearing obligations of the United States or in obligations guaranteed as to both principal and interest by the United States.[9] Investing the payroll tax revenues for even a few days ensures that the trust funds maximize interest income. Under the terms of this exchange, when Treasury credits payroll tax and other revenues to Social Security in the form of certificates of indebtedness (CIs), the revenues themselves become available in the general fund for other government operations. The securities that the Treasury issues to the Social Security trust funds count toward the federal debt limit.[10]

Social Security benefits are paid by the Treasury using cash from the general fund. If Treasury lacks sufficient cash on hand to pay benefits, it must borrow by issuing new public debt. When Treasury pays Social Security benefits, it redeems an equivalent amount of Treasury securities held by the trust funds in order to reimburse the general fund.

The Social Security program is projected to run a cash deficit in FY2011. That is, Social Security's outlays for benefit payments and administration are projected to exceed its tax revenues. In a year when Social Security runs a cash flow deficit, the Treasury redeems additional government securities held by the trust funds.

Social Security financial operations have been slightly modified to accommodate a temporary reduction in Social Security payroll taxes for employees and the self-employed. The Tax Relief, Unemployment Insurance Reauthorization, and Job Creation Act of 2010 (P.L. 111-312, signed on December 17, 2010), among other provisions, provides a temporary two percentage point reduction in the Social Security payroll tax for employees and the self-employed in 2011, resulting in a tax rate of 4.2% for employees and 10.4% for the self-employed. To protect the Social Security trust funds from a loss of payroll tax revenues, P.L. 111-312 appropriates to the Social Security trust funds amounts equal to the reduction in revenues to the Treasury.[11]

The Social Security trust funds receive interest payments in the form of additional securities from the U.S. Treasury each June 30 and December 31.[12] In other words, Treasury is obligated to issue additional debt, that is subject to limit, twice a year in order to pay interest to the Social Security and certain other trust funds. When federal debt is near its statutory limit, making those interest payments could pose a challenge to Treasury debt and cash management operations.

The Social Security trust funds were designed to provide financial resources to pay future benefits. The federal government, however, must raise revenues, cut spending, or borrow in order to obtain funds that will allow the U.S. Treasury to redeem the trust fund securities in the future. If Treasury obtained funds to redeem trust fund securities by borrowing an equivalent amount from the public, then intragovernmental debt would in effect be converted into debt held by the public, so that the net impact on total federal debt would be zero.[13]

If the federal government were running a budget surplus, and therefore had a positive cash balance in Treasury's general fund, Treasury could redeem the trust fund assets by using surplus cash. Trust fund balances would fall, but there would be no increase in debt held by the public. The net impact would be to reduce total federal debt. If those future redemptions of securities held by the Social Security trust funds were financed by cutting support for federal programs or raising taxes, then program beneficiaries and taxpayers at that time would bear an indirect burden of supporting Social Security benefits.

Debt Limit[14]

Nearly all federal debt is subject to a statutory limit.[15] The current debt limit was set in February 2010 (P.L. 111-139) at $14,294 billion. The federal debt limit has been raised 16 times since 1993. On April 29, 2011, debt subject to the debt limit was $14,236 billion, about $58 billion below the current statutory debt limit.

The U.S. Treasury projects the federal debt will reach its statutory limit before May 16, 2011. Treasury Secretary Timothy Geithner, in a letter to Congress dated May 2, 2011, wrote that he would declare a debt issuance suspension period on May 16, unless Congress acted beforehand, which would allow certain extraordinary measures to Treasury's borrowing capacity until early August 2011.[16] That letter, the third sent by the Treasury Secretary since January 2011, noted that funding federal operations could soon become complicated without a debt limit increase. Certain measures that rely on the Treasury Secretary's existing authority, such as the draw-down of the Supplementary Financing Program, are underway.

New issues of State and Local Government Series (SLGS) Treasury securities, according to the May 2 letter, were scheduled for suspension on May 6, 2011. On that date, Treasury announced that it had suspended issue of SLGSs until further notice. SLGSs help state and local governments satisfy federal requirements designed to prohibit tax arbitrage of proceeds of bond issues enjoying certain exemptions from federal taxation.[17]

The U.S. Treasury had previously estimated the debt limit would be reached between April 15 and May 31, 2011, with extraordinary measures projected to extend Treasury's ability to borrow until about July 8, 2011.[18] The U.S. Treasury may face severe difficulties in funding federal operations in late July or early August without a debt limit increase.[19]

Deficits, Debt, and Interest Costs

This section discusses the relationships among federal deficits, debt, and interest costs. A deficit or surplus is the annual flow of revenues minus the flow of outlays, which accumulates into a stock of debt. Net interest costs are the flow of payments that compensate investors and nonfederal organizations for holding federal debt.

Deficits and the Accumulation of Federal Debt

Federal debt held by the public is essentially the sum of federal budget deficits over time. The annual federal deficit, however, will not exactly equal the year-over-year increase in federal debt due to certain technical adjustments.[20] Over the long term, however, the cumulative size of deficits determines the magnitude of the federal debt.

Each year, the U.S. Office of Management and Budget (OMB) provides a reconciliation between the federal deficit and the increase in the federal debt. The first major adjustment reflects the treatment of federal credit programs. The Federal Credit Reform Act (FCRA) requires that the net subsidy costs (rather than year-by-year cash flows) be used to assess the budgetary costs of federal loan and loan guarantee programs.[21] Troubled Asset Relief Program (TARP) costs are scored on a FCRA basis, but include risk adjustments.[22] While many budget experts consider FCRA a step toward sound accrual accounting of federal credit programs, the year-by-year cash flows are what affect federal borrowing requirements. Thus, an adjustment is needed to account for the difference between the FCRA-mandated accrual treatment of loan and loan guarantee programs and the year-by-year actual cash flows that affect Treasury debt management operations. The second major adjustment reflects gains from seniorage, which results from the difference between the cost of minting coins and their face value.

The federal government also may face other potential liabilities not reflected in current federal budget concepts. For example, federal credit accounting may understate the costs of financial risks to the federal government. In particular, the deprivatization of the mortgage giants Fannie Mae and Freddie Mac may expose the federal government to significant financial risks.[23]

The Federal Debt over Time

For most of the history of the United States, federal debt was closely linked to war finance. In more recent decades, the growing costs of federally financed health care and other entitlement spending have played an important role in the government's fiscal situation. Higher spending on defense and other security costs, as well as tax cuts and other tax policy decisions, have also influenced the size of federal deficits and the accumulation of debt. Figure 2 shows federal deficits and surpluses since 1929 as a percentage of GDP.

The federal government ran very large deficits during the 1940s—hitting 30% of GDP in 1943— to finance military activities during World War II. Deficit finance, however, played little role in funding the Korean War or the early stages of the Vietnam War.[24] In the 1970s, deficits as a share of GDP grew as economic growth slowed due to sharp increases in oil and other commodity prices, slower productivity growth, turmoil in the international financial system, expanded regulatory activity, and stiffer competition in international product markets, while federal spending due to health care and other domestic programs grew faster than federal revenues. In the 1980s, cuts in domestic programs were too small to offset large tax cuts and increases in military spending, which led to large increases in federal deficits.[25]

In 1985, Congress passed the Balanced Budget and Emergency Deficit Control Act of 1985 (P.L. 99-177), informally known as Gramm-Rudman-Hollings (GRH), which introduced triggers for automatic budget cuts called *sequesters* if certain deficit targets were not met, along with other budget enforcement mechanisms. The GRH framework was modified several times in the late 1980s. In the fall of 1990, congressional leaders and President George H.W. Bush engaged in a series of budget negotiations at Andrews Air Force Base that set the framework for the Omnibus Budget Reconciliation Act of 1990 (P.L. 101-508). That measure included discretionary spending caps, modifications to entitlement programs, and tax increases, along with changes in the budgetary treatment of loan and loan guarantee programs (see discussion of FCRA above) among other provisions.[26]

The collapse in 1989 of most of the Warsaw Pact governments in Central and Eastern Europe and the 1990-1991 disintegration of the Soviet Union was followed by a reduction in federal defense spending, allowing a "peace dividend" that relaxed fiscal pressures.[27] In addition, strong economic growth, further modifications of certain entitlement programs, and tax increases led to four years of federal budget surpluses from FY1998 through FY2001.

The attacks on the World Trade Center towers in New York and on the Pentagon on September 11, 2001, were followed by sharp increases in homeland security spending. Defense spending also increased dramatically with the start of the Afghanistan war in October 2001 and the Iraq war in March 2003.[28] Major tax cuts in 2001 and 2003 reduced federal receipts below baseline levels.[29] Federal surpluses, which had been predicted to last throughout the decade, quickly turned to deficits in the face of the "dot-com" recession of 2000-2001, large tax cuts, the expiration of certain budget enforcement mechanisms in 2002, homeland security and defense costs, and the creation of new federal benefits (i.e., Medicare Prescription Drug, Improvement, and Modernization Act of 2003; P.L. 108-173).[30] In addition, rising health care costs and rising numbers of retirees continued to push up costs for federal programs such as Medicare.

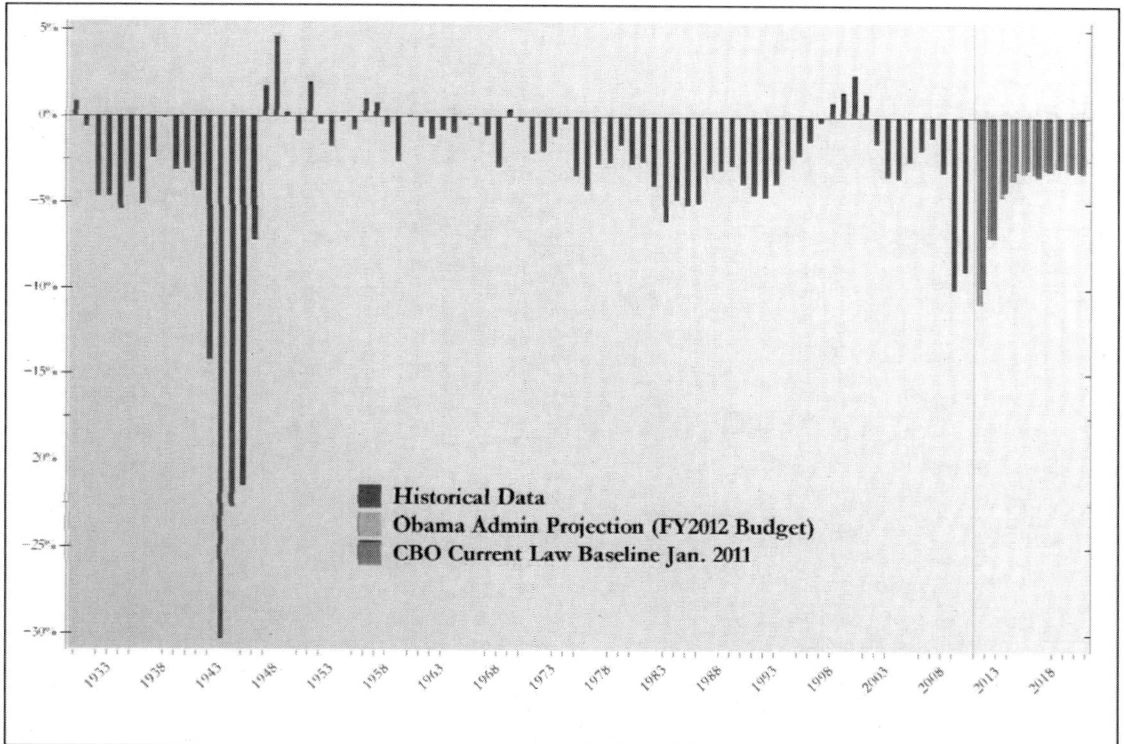

Source: CRS analysis of OMB and CBO data and projections. Administrative budget concepts used for pre-1933 data, rather than Unified budget concepts. Notes: Data for FY2011 are estimated and later years are projected. Transition quarter (1976) omitted.

Figure 2. United States Government Budget Surplus or Deficit; FY1929-FY2021, as a percentage of GDP.

The financial crisis of 2007-2008 and the subsequent recession led to major decreases in federal receipts and sharp spending increases for many federal programs, some due to "automatic stabilizer" effects. As incomes of many families shrank, more became eligible to receive help from federal and state income security programs. In addition, the American Recovery and Reinvestment Act of 2009 (P.L. 111-5), which was designed to stimulate the economy by increasing the deficit, provided support for state and local governments, increased spending on certain federal programs, and reduced tax revenues.

Deficits over the next few years are expected to drop sharply as the economy recovers. Many economists remain concerned that economic growth may be slow for several years, and that the retirement of baby boom cohorts combined with persistent increases in per-beneficiary medical costs will continue to present daunting fiscal challenges to policymakers.

Interest Costs

Interest rates on federal debt have fallen to extremely low levels by historical standards, in large part due to the effects of the 2007-2008 financial crises and subsequent recession.[31] Thus, even though total federal debt as well as federal debt held by the public has increased sharply, interest costs as a proportion of the budget have remained relatively low for the past few years.[32] Figure 3 shows federal net interest costs as a proportion of gross domestic product (GDP).

Payments from one part of the federal government to another net to zero for government-wide totals. Thus, most analyses of the budgetary effects of federal interest costs ignore intragovernmental interest payments, and focus on net interest payments.

Net federal interest costs are projected to rise rapidly. As business activities return to normal levels, demand for loans increases, pushing up interest rates—a typical consequence of economic recovery. For this reason, most forecasters expect interest rates to rise over the next few years. Federal debt levels, according to CBO, OMB, and private forecasts, will continue to increase in coming years.

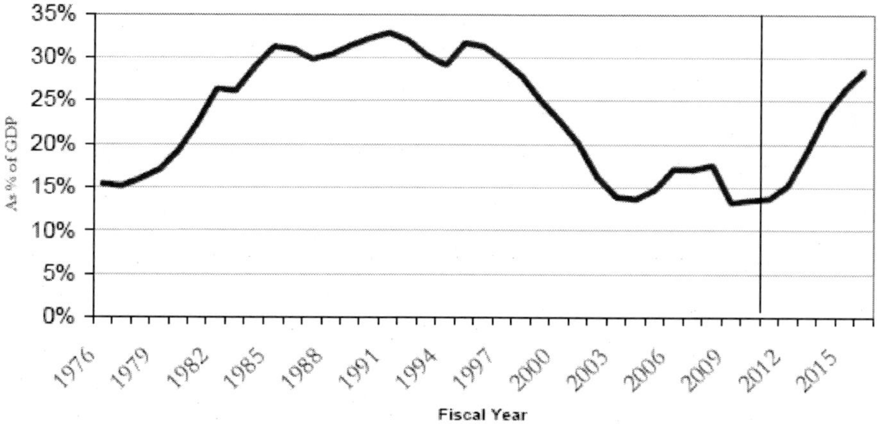

Source: OMB, Budget for FY2012, *Historical Tables*.

Notes: Transition quarter omitted. FY2011 costs are estimated, FY2012-FY2016 reflect President's proposals.

Figure 3. Federal Net Interest Costs as a Percentage of GDP; FY1976-FY2016.

Federal debt service costs, which can be expressed as the total federal debt held by the public multiplied by the average interest rate on that debt, are therefore expected to rise sharply over the next decade. According to April 2011 CBO baseline projections, net interest costs will rise from $213 billion in FY2011 to $534 billion in FY2016, and are projected to reach $807 billion in FY2021. Because interest rates are currently at low levels, the percentage increase in future interest rates will probably exceed the percentage increase in debt levels.[33] Growing interest payments would put pressure on public resources, requiring either spending reductions, revenue increases, or higher borrowing levels, or some combination of those. Financing interest payments by borrowing, rather than through spending reductions or revenue increases, accelerates the accumulation of debt, which would lead to higher interest costs and could result in heightened rollover risks—that is, the risk that bond markets become reluctant to buy new debt instruments issued to finance the redemption of old or maturing debt instruments.

Rising interest rates affect the federal government's finances in several ways. Higher interest rates translate into higher debt service costs to compensate private investors for holding government debt, as well as higher interest payments to federal trust funds. U.S. Treasury interest payments to federal trust funds generally net out, as interest owed by the U.S. Treasury (counted as a liability) is counterbalanced by the income due (counted as an asset) to the trust funds. Higher interest income earned by the federal trust funds, however, would tend to strengthen the financial situation of federal programs linked to trust funds such as Medicare and Social Security. On the other hand, when higher interest rates or other income increase trust fund balances, the sums that the U.S. Treasury will ultimately be obliged to redeem also increase. Finally, higher interest rates, other things equal, may affect surpluses generated by the Federal Reserve System, which are then transferred to the U.S. Treasury. The magnitude of the Federal Reserve's balance sheet, which expanded substantially in the wake of the 2007-2008 financial crisis, and the non-traditional nature of some items on that balance sheet, could complicate efforts to estimate how interest rate changes would affect the Federal Reserve's finances.

CBO has recently run some sensitivity analyses of federal interest costs. In January 2011, CBO estimated that a 1-point increase in interest rates above baseline projection levels would increase federal net interest costs by $15 billion in FY2011 and $438 billion over the FY2012-FY2016 budget window, assuming other economic variables were held equal.[34] CBO also projected that a 0.1-point increase in interest rates above baseline levels would lead to a relatively small change in interest costs for FY2011 and a $5 billion increase in debt service costs over the FY2012-FY2016 period. In February 2011, CBO calculated how projected federal interest costs would respond in three scenarios. In each scenario, interest rates would rise above CBO baseline levels, and thus would lead to higher projected interest costs.[35]

Interest Rates on Short-Term and Long-Term Debt

Yields on fixed income securities, such as Treasury securities, are tied to market interest rates. Interest rates on short-term variable-rate securities are typically lower than interest rates on longterm fixed-rate securities, because investors usually require compensation to bear interest-rate risks embedded in long-maturity assets.[36] From a borrower's point of view, raising funds using longer-term securities is more expensive, but in effect provides some insurance against future interest rate increases. Figure 3 shows interest rates for 3-month, 1-year, and 10-year Treasury securities.

The relationship between interest rates and maturities is often called the yield curve. The yield curve normally slopes upward, reflecting the need to compensate holders of longer-term securities with higher interest rates. In some unusual circumstances, the yield curve may flatten or even invert.

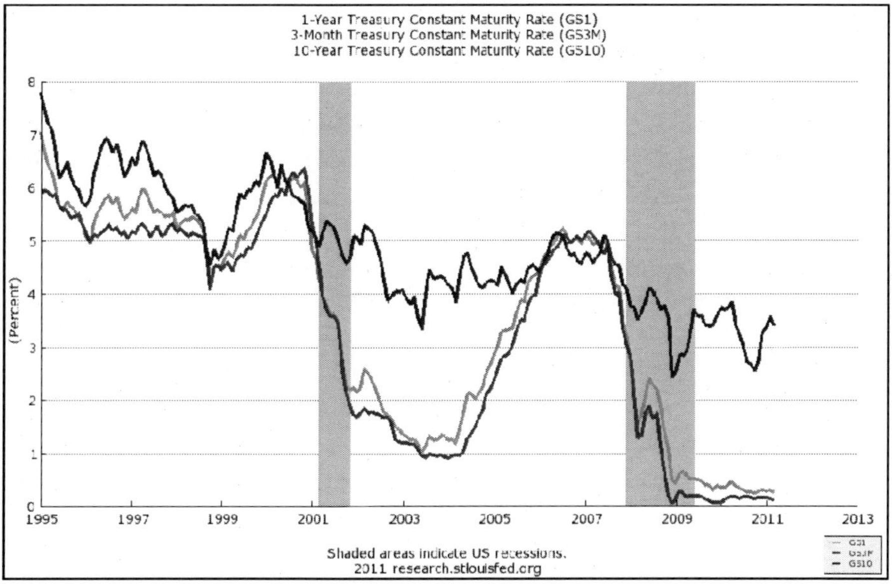

Source: St. Louis Federal Reserve Bank.
Notes: Top line is 10-year rate, bottom is 3-month rate.

Figure 4. Interest Rates for Selected Treasury Securities by Maturity; January 1995-March 2011.

HOLDINGS OF FEDERAL DEBT

This section describes the maturity structure of the federal debt, that is, the mix of short-, medium-, and long-term Treasury securities. This section also looks at what types of investors hold federal debt.[37]

Maturity Structure of the Federal Debt

Figure 4 shows trends in the average maturity of federal securities over the second half of the 20th century. Long-term securities financed a large proportion of the costs of military operations during World War II. As the federal debt was paid down during the 1950s and 1960s, however, average maturity of Treasury debt fell. In the 1970s, rising inflation rates made longer-term securities less attractive, and average maturity of Treasury securities fell to two years and five months in December 1975. Average maturities then rose to about six years by the late 1980s. In 2001, average maturities began to fall, in part due to the discontinuance of the 30-year bond, colloquially known as the "long bond." The U.S. Treasury, however, brought the long bond back in 2006, in part due to demand by institutional investors with long-term liabilities, such as insurers, and in part due to reduced yields on long-term securities, which made them a more attractive means of financing debt.[38]

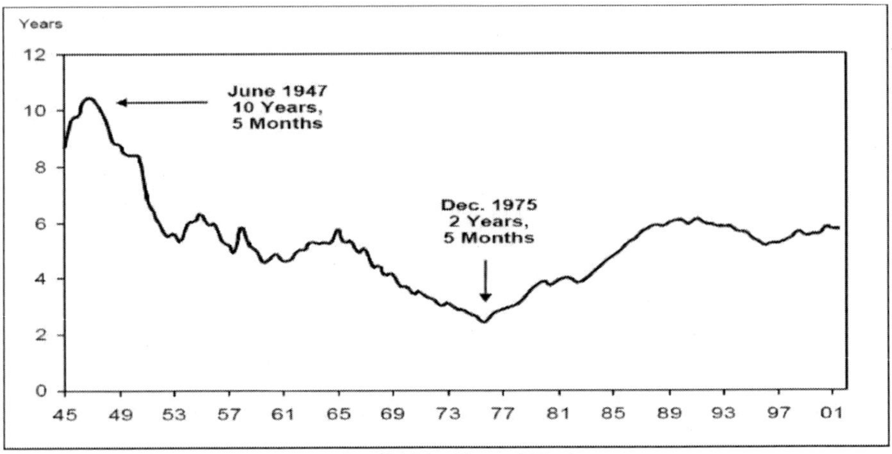

Source: *Treasury Bulletin*, December 2001, Charts FD-A.

Figure 5. Average Maturity of Privately Held U.S. Marketable Debt, 1945-2001.

Figure 5 shows trends in the maturity composition of privately held marketable Treasury debt and Figure 6 shows trends in its average maturity since 1999. After 2001, when average maturity of Treasury securities reached six years, the average maturity of Treasury debt held by the public fell gradually until 2008, signaling an increased reliance on shorter-term securities to finance federal deficits.

The financial crisis and subsequent recession increased federal borrowing requirements sharply, as the proportion of short-term Treasury securities rose more quickly than longer-term securities. Issuing short-term securities, rather than longer-term securities, may have provided an operationally less complex way to meet borrowing requirements in tumultuous financial conditions. In addition, those tempestuous financial conditions of late 2008 may have reduced demand for longer-term securities, which could have helped push down the average maturity of Treasury securities. In late 2008, average maturity for Treasury debt shortened to less than four years. The maturity composition and average maturity of Treasury debt, however, have rebounded to more normal levels by 2010, as Treasury rebalanced its security offerings.

Some market observers expressed concerns about the shortening of average Treasury debt maturities and applauded the lengthening of average Treasury maturity in 2010.[39] Shorter average Treasury maturities could raise three concerns. Many institutional investors, such as pension and insurance companies, demand long-term debt instruments that help them manage long-term liabilities. A reduction in the share of long-term Treasury debt instruments relative to short-term instruments might complicate portfolio management of such investors. Second, borrowers who depend more on longer-term debt instruments are less vulnerable to the risk of rising interest rates. Third, using a greater proportion of long-term debt instruments reduces rollover risks.

Ownership of Publicly Held Debt

A growing proportion of the federal debt is held by foreign investors and governments.[40] Figure 7 shows how holdings of interest-bearing Treasury debt are distributed among investors and organizations around the world according to January 2011 U.S. Treasury estimates.[41] At the end of February 2011, the U.S. Treasury issued revised figures, which showed larger holdings of Treasury securities by the People's Republic of China and smaller holdings in some other countries, such as the United Kingdom.[42] Figure 8 shows changes in ownership of the publicly held federal debt by country since 1990.

Foreign holdings of federal debt have increased for several reasons. First, global capital markets have become more international since the 1970s, when regulatory controls on the capital flows were common. In addition, many international investors have diversified their portfolios by including assets from many different countries. Second, some countries, especially in East Asia, have had very high savings rates that have financed significant accumulations of federal debt. By contrast, savings rates for the United States have been relatively low in recent decades, although savings rates have increased in the wake of the 2007-2008 financial crisis. Third, trade and budget deficits that emerged in the 1980s implied that the flow of goods to the United States was in part financed by the flow of assets, public and private, to countries with trade surpluses.

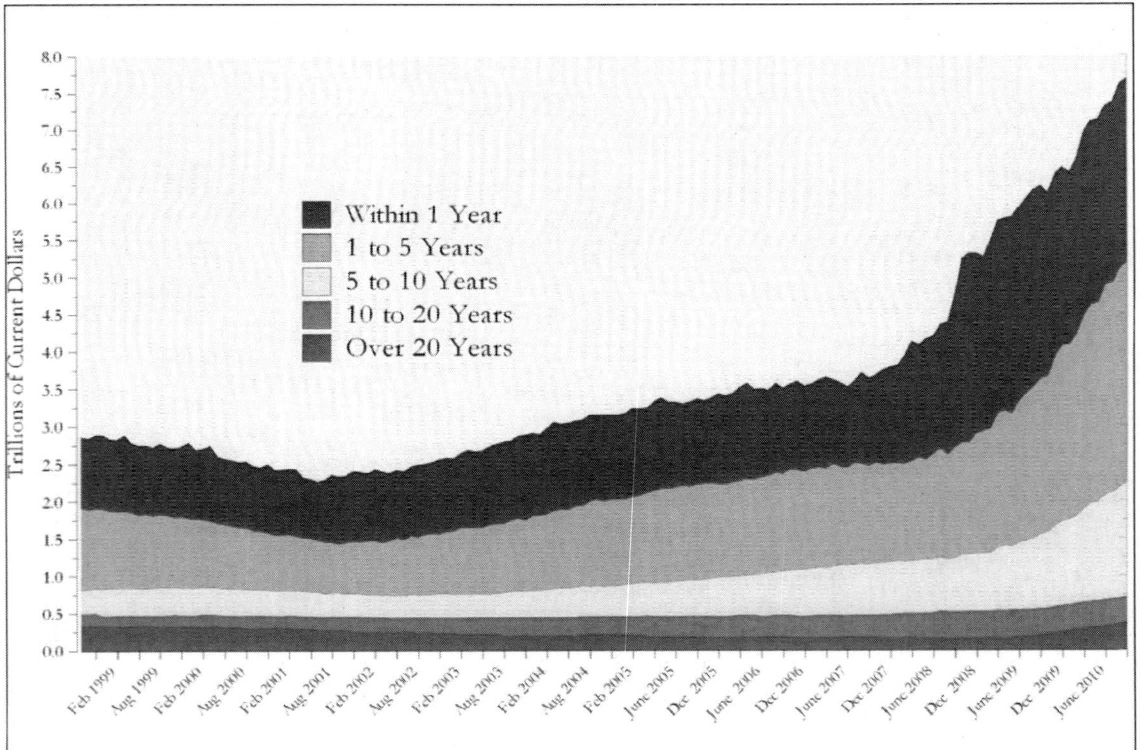

Source: CRS analysis of U.S. Treasury data (Treasury Bulletin, Table FD-5, various issues). Figure by Andrew Austin, CRS.

Figure 6. Composition of Privately Held U.S. Marketable Interest-Bearing Public Debt By Maturity Class; Monthly averages, September 1998-September 2010.

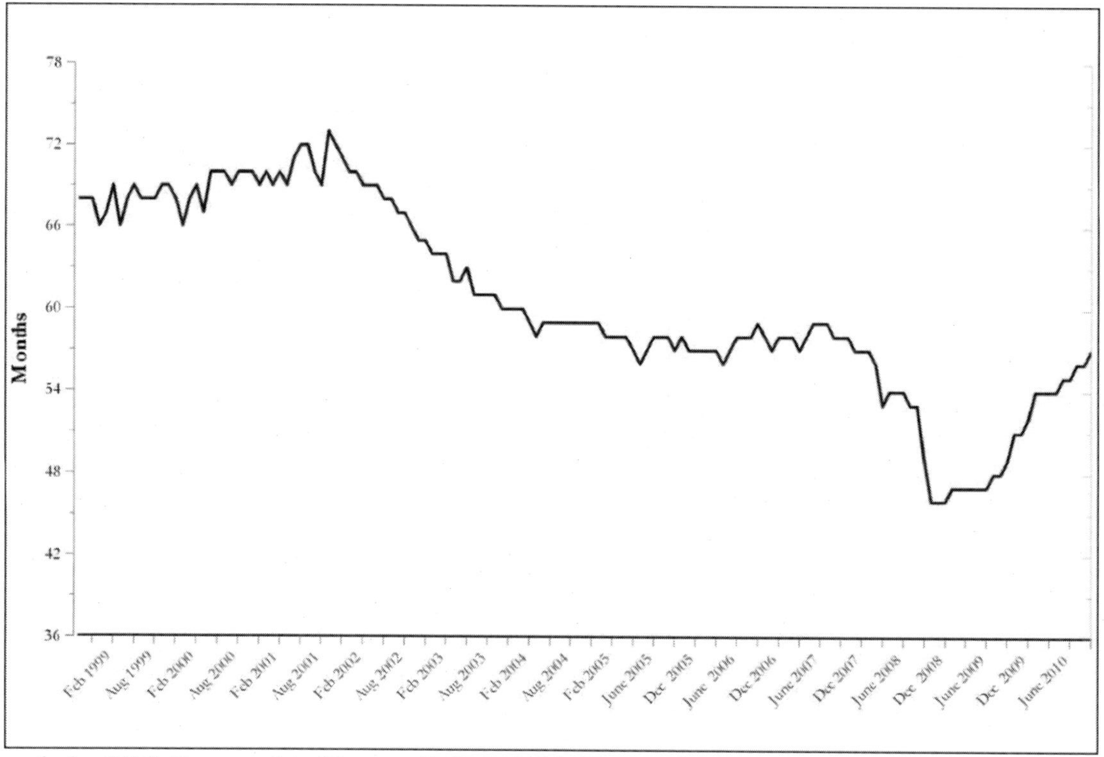

Source: CRS analysis of U.S. Treasury data (Treasury Bulletin, Table FD-5, various issues). Figure by Andrew Austin, CRS.

Figure 7. Average Maturity of Privately Held U.S. Marketable Interest-Bearing Public Debt; Monthly averages, September 1998-September 2010.

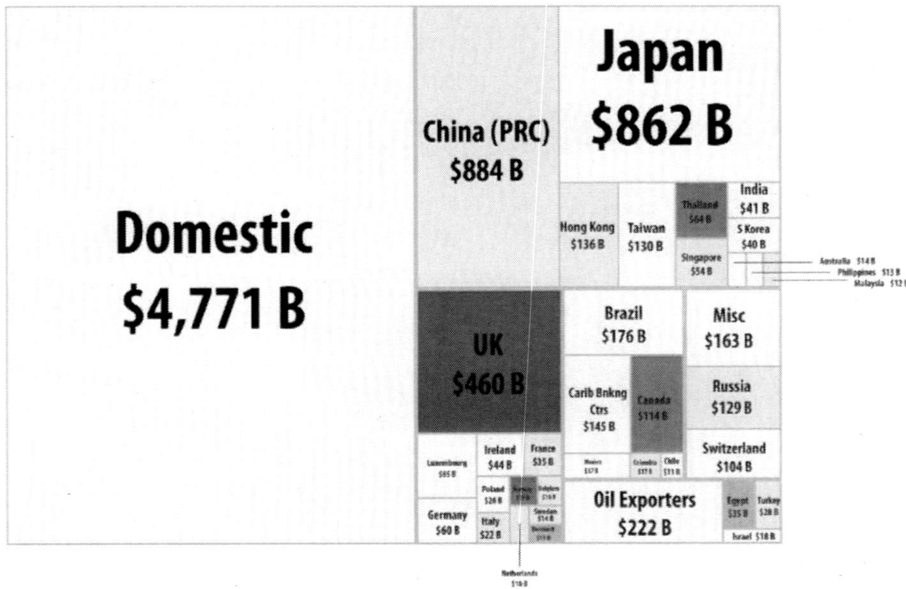

Source: CRS, based on data obtained from Treasury International Capital System (http://www.treasury.gov/resource-center/data-chart-center/tic/Pages/index.aspx), January 2011 release.

Notes: Color reflects increases (blue) and decreases (pink) in holdings since November 2009. United Kingdom includes Channel Islands and Isle of Man. Oil Exporters includes Ecuador, Venezuela, Indonesia, Bahrain, Iran, Iraq, Kuwait, Oman, Qatar, Saudi Arabia, the United Arab Emirates, Algeria, Gabon, Libya, and Nigeria. Caribbean Banking Centers include Bahamas, Bermuda, British Virgin Islands, Cayman Islands, Netherlands Antilles and Panama. China (PRC) excludes Hong Kong and Macau, which are reported separately. See source for additional notes.

Figure 8. Holdings of Interest-Bearing U.S. Treasury Securities by Country; $Billions, as of September 2010.

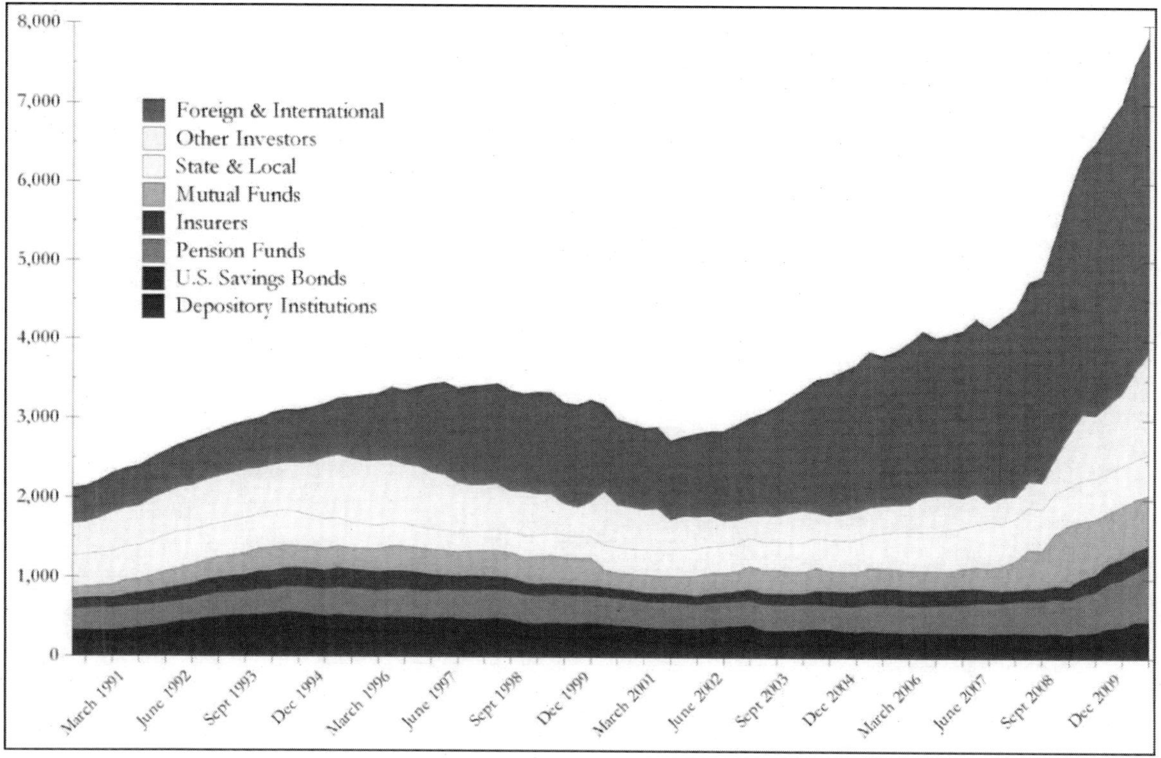

Source: CRS, based on data from U.S. Treasury, *Treasury Bulletin*, various issues, Table OFS-2.

Notes: Other investors category includes individuals, government-sponsored enterprises, brokers and dealers, bank personal trusts and estates, corporate and non-corporate businesses, and other investors.

Figure 9. Holdings of U.S. Treasury Securities By Type of Investor; $Billions.

Some concerns have been expressed that large federal debt holdings by the People's Republic of China (PRC) could be used to exert political or financial leverage to influence international capital markets or U.S. foreign policy. The Chinese government has sought to allay such concerns by stating that it would not dump holdings of Treasury securities.[43] Some China analysts, however, have expressed concern about rising inventories of U.S. Treasury debt.[44] Shifts in the PRC's exchange rate policies could affect its demand for U.S. Treasury securities.[45]

WHAT IS THE "BEST" MEASURE OF FEDERAL DEBT?

Measures of federal debt, because they represent accumulated deficits over time, are backward-looking measures of the government's fiscal condition. Some forward-looking measures of the federal debt may more accurately reflect the federal government's fiscal condition and its ability to face future budgetary challenges.[46]

Factors expected to affect future federal outlays and receipts, including demographic structure, design of major mandatory spending programs such as Medicare and Medicaid, and the growth of health care costs, may all have important consequences on future budgets. Federal debt and the costs of servicing in some projection scenarios generate feedback effects that could reduce the sustainability of debt burdens. For example, higher debt servicing requirements could put upward pressure on interest rates, which could crowd out private investment, which, in turn, would slow economic growth, thus reducing the economy's ability to finance government activities.

Some contend that commonly used measures of federal debt within the current system of budget concepts have some important limitations.[47] Federal budget concepts generally adhere to a cash basis, rather than an accrual basis used by many firms. Accrual accounting, in which liabilities and assets are recognized when taken on, rather than when funds are acquired or disbursed, has some advantages for medium- and long-term financial planning. The federal government does use a modified form of accrual accounting for loan and loan guarantee programs since passage of the Federal Credit Reform Act (FCRA) as well as for certain federal retirement programs.[48]

A wider use of accrual accounting could pose thorny problems for federal financial management, however. Accrual accounting methods necessarily involve complex judgments of future cost and revenue streams. Because the information and knowledge to make those decisions often resides deep within federal agencies, the ability to make such accrual accounting decisions could give agencies greater flexibility to shift budgetary resources among programs and time periods, which could undermine the OMB's ability to exercise tight budgetary controls and Congress's ability to control spending,[49]

Federal debt concepts such as total debt and debt held by the public are not netted against assets held by the federal government. In the wake of financial interventions undertaken in 2007-2008, the U.S. government acquired substantial assets. For example, the federal government acquired financial assets in return for support from the Troubled Asset Relief Program (TARP), through the deprivatization of mortgage giants Fannie Mae and Freddie Mac, and in other ways. OMB and CBO in recent years have presented calculations of federal debt net of financial assets to reflect those holdings. Recent financial statements of the U.S. government issued by the U.S. Treasury also present some estimates of the value of "heritage assets," as well as certain unfunded liabilities not reflected in current federal budget concepts.[50]

One forward-looking measure of fiscal condition is the *fiscal gap*. A fiscal gap represents the size of fiscal adjustment, either though spending reductions or revenue increases or a combination of both, that would stabilize the ratio of debt to GDP. CBO, as well as other organizations, computes fiscal gap estimates for the federal government. The latest CBO long-term calculations estimated the 75-year fiscal gap at about 0.7% of GDP under an "Extended Baseline" scenario and at 8.7% of GDP under an "Alternative Fiscal Scenario."[51] Many budget analysts consider the more optimistic "Extended Baseline" projections less realistic than the more pessimistic "Alternative Fiscal Scenario."

CONCLUSION

The federal government's ability to borrow at relatively low interest rates allows it to shift buying power backwards and forwards through time, in order to support macroeconomic policy goals and lessen financial shocks borne by citizens.[52] The reputation of federal debt as one of the safest investments possible allows Treasury securities to play a central role in financial markets. On the other hand, a growing federal debt could place a high burden on future generations and hinder economic growth. Rapid growth of federal debt could also increase the probability of a financial crisis or fears of a sovereign default.[53]

The future trajectory of federal spending and revenues implied by current law and expected economic conditions, according to many respected organizations, implies that the federal government will face increasingly difficult fiscal challenges. Finding ways to stabilize the federal growth has therefore become a prominent concern of policymakers.

End Notes

[1] See also U.S. Congressional Budget Office (CBO), *Federal Debt and Interest Costs*, December 2010, available at http://www.cbo.gov/doc.cfm?index=11999&zzz=41471.

[2] At the end of March 1, 2011, total federal debt outstanding was $14,173 billion. Debt held by the public was $9,563 billion and intragovernmental debt as $4,610 billion.

[3] CRS Report R40767, *How Treasury Issues Debt*, by Mindy R. Levit.

[4] For more information see U.S. Treasury, "SLGS FAQ," available at http://www.treasurydirect.gov/govt/resources/ faq/faq_slgs.htm.

[5] For more information, see CRS Report R41811, *State and Local Government Series (SLGS) Treasury Debt: A Description*, by Steven Maguire; and U.S. Treasury, "SLGS FAQ," available at http://www.treasurydirect.gov/govt/ resources/faq/faq_slgs.htm.

[6] Alison Shelton (CRS/Domestic Social Policy Division) contributed to the discussion of Social Security finance.

[7] For details of federal trust funds and federal fund accounts, see U.S. Office of Management and Budget, *FY2011 Budget of the U.S. Government, Analytic Perspectives*, ch. 27. See also U.S. Congressional Budget Office, *Budget and Economic Outlook*, Appendix C, January 2011, available at http://www.cbo.gov/ftpdocs/120xx/doc12039/01-26_FY2011Outlook.pdf.

[8] CRS Report R41328, *Federal Trust Funds and the Budget*, by Thomas L. Hungerford.

[9] 42 U.S.C. § 401(d).

[10] U.S. Government Accounting Office, *Treasury's Management of Social Security Trust Funds During the Debt Ceiling Crises* (GAO/HRD-86-45), December 5, 1985, available at http://archive.gao.gov/d12t3/128621.pdf.

[11] The law specifies that these appropriated amounts "shall be transferred from the general fund at such times and in such manner as to replicate to the extent possible the transfers which would have occurred to such Trust Fund had such amendments not been enacted."

[12] The Medicare trust funds, specifically the Hospital Insurance (HI; Part A) and Supplemental Medical Insurance (Parts B and D) trust funds, as well as the Civil Service Retirement and Disability Fund (CSRDF) also receive interest payments on the June/December schedule.

[13] In a situation where there is a budget surplus and therefore a positive cash balance in Treasury's general fund, Treasury could redeem the trust fund assets by using surplus cash, and then the trust fund balance would fall but there would be no increase in debt held by the public. The net impact would be to reduce total federal debt.

[14] For details, see CRS Report RL31967, *The Debt Limit: History and Recent Increases*, by D. Andrew Austin and Mindy R. Levit.

[15] The total debt outstanding data available at the U.S. Treasury's Bureau of the Public Debt "Debt to the Penny" website is not the debt subject to limit (http://www.treasurydirect.gov/ NP/BPDLogin?application=np). Debt subject to limit, and its relation to total debt outstanding, is shown in Table III-C of the *Daily Treasury Statement*, available at http://fms.treas.gov/dts/index.html.

[16] Secretary of the U.S. Treasury Timothy Geithner, letter to Speaker John Boehner, dated May 2, 2011, available: http://www.treasury.gov/connect/blog/Documents/FINAL%20Debt% 20Limit%20Letter%2005-02- 2011%20Boehner.pdf. The same text was sent to all Members.

[17] For more information, see CRS Report R41811, *State and Local Government Series (SLGS) Treasury Debt: A Description*, by Steven Maguire; and U.S. Treasury, "SLGS FAQ," available at http://www.treasurydirect.gov/govt/ resources/faq/faq_slgs.htm.

[18] Secretary of the U.S. Treasury Timothy Geithner, letter to Majority Leader Harry Reid, dated April 4, 2011, available at http://www.treasury.gov/connect/blog/Documents/FINAL%20Letter%2004-04-2011%20Reid%20Debt%20Limit.pdf; U.S. Treasury, "Treasury Issues Updated Debt Limit Projections," March 1, 2011, available at http://www.treasury.gov/press-center/press-releases/Pages/tg1084.aspx.

[19] See CRS Report R41633, *Reaching the Debt Limit: Background and Potential Effects on Government Operations*, coordinated by Mindy R. Levit.

[20] See Table 6-2 "Federal Government Financing and Debt" in the *Analytic Perspectives* volume (p. 62) of the President's FY2012 budget submission, available at http://www. whitehouse.gov/sites/default/files/omb/budget/fy2012/ assets/econ_analyses.pdf.

[21] FCRA was established by Title V of the Omnibus Budget Reconciliation Act of 1990 (P.L. 101-508). See CRS Report RL30346, *Federal Credit Reform: Implementation of the Changed Budgetary Treatment of Direct Loans and Loan Guarantees*, by James M. Bickley.

[22] Section 123 of the Emergency Economic Stabilization Act of 2008 (EESA; Division A of P.L. 110-343).

[23] Deborah J. Lucas and Marvin Phaup, "Reforming Credit Reform," *Public Budgeting & Finance*, vol. 28, no. 4 (winter 2008), pp. 90-110.

[24] For a history of deficit finance and American wars, see Robert D. Hormats, *The Price of Liberty*, (New York: Times Books, 2007). Also see CRS Report RL31176, *Financing Issues and Economic Effects of American Wars*, by Marc Labonte and Mindy R. Levit.

[25] For one view of budgetary politics in the early 1980s, see David Stockman, *The Triumph of Politics*, (New York: Harper & Row, 1986).

[26] President George H.W. Bush, "Statement on Signing the Omnibus Budget Reconciliation Act of 1990," November 5, 1990, available at http://www.presidency.ucsb.edu/ws/index.php?pid=19000.

[27] The Warsaw Treaty Organization, established in 1955, included Albania, Bulgaria, Czechoslovakia, the German Democratic Republic, Hungary, Poland, Romania, and the Soviet Union.

[28] CRS Report RL33110, *The Cost of Iraq, Afghanistan, and Other Global War on Terror Operations Since 9/11*, by Amy Belasco.

[29] CRS Report R41393, *The Bush Tax Cuts and the Economy*, by Thomas L. Hungerford.

[30] For details, see CRS Report R41134, *The Impact of Major Legislation on Budget Deficits: 2001 to 2009*, by Marc Labonte.

[31] Congressional Budget Office, *Federal Debt and Interest Costs*, Dec. 2010, available at http://www.cbo.gov/doc.cfm?index=11999&zzz=41471.

[32] See CRS Report RS22354, *Interest Payments on the Federal Debt: A Primer*, by Thomas L. Hungerford.

[33] U.S. Congressional Budget Office, *An Analysis of the President's Budgetary Proposals for Fiscal Year 2012,* April 15, 2011, Table 1-5, available at http://www.cbo.gov/ doc.cfm?index=12130.

[34] CBO, *Budget and Economic Outlook*, January 2011, Appendix B, available at http://www.cbo.gov/ftpdocs/120xx/doc12039/01-26_FY2011Outlook.pdf.

[35] Douglas W. Elmendorf, CBO Director, letter to House Budget Committee Chairman Paul Ryan, dated February 24, 2011, available at

http://www.cbo.gov/ftpdocs/120xx/doc12081/Ryan_Letter_Interest_Rates_2-24-2011.pdf.

[36] An investor who buys a long-term security cannot react to changing circumstances until the security matures or is sold. In financial terms, when an investor buys a long-term asset, she forgoes "option value," which is the value of being able to react to new information or conditions. In a competitive market, the asset's yield relative to a short-term alternative will reflect the expected value of that forgone option value.

[37] See also CRS Report RL34682, *Federal Debt Management: Concepts, Options, and Policies (1945-2008)*, by James M. Bickley.

[38] U.S. Treasury, TreasuryDirect, "Treasury Reintroduces 30-Year Bond," January 2006, available at http://www.treasurydirect.gov/indiv/research/articles/res_invest_articles_30yearbondarticle_0106.htm.

[39] Report to the Secretary of the Treasury from the Treasury Borrowing Advisory Committee of the Securities Industry and Financial Markets Association (SIFMA), February 1, 2011, available at http://www.treasury.gov/press-center/ press-releases/Pages/tg1047.aspx.

[40] CRS Report RS22331, *Foreign Holdings of Federal Debt*, by Justin Murray and Marc Labonte. See also the U.S. Treasury International Capital System website at http://www.treasury.gov/resource-center/data-chart-enter/tic/Pages/ index.aspx.

[41] For details on estimation methods, see Carol C. Bertaut, William Griever, and Ralph W. Tryon, "Understanding U.S. Cross-Border Securities Data," in *Federal Reserve Bulletin*, May 4, 2006, pp. A59-75, available at http://www.treasury.gov/resource-center/data-chart-center/tic/Documents/frbul2006.pdf.

[42] U.S. Treasury, "Preliminary Report on Foreign Holdings of U.S. Securities at End-June 2010," February 28, 2011, available at http://www.treasury.gov/press-center/press-releases/Pages/tg1079.aspx.

[43] Geoff Dyer and Peter Garnham, "Beijing Rules Out 'Nuclear Option' of Dumping Holdings of U.S. Bonds,:" *Financial Times*, July 6, 2010, p. 1.

[44] Howard Schneider, "China's $3 Trillion Dilemma: What to Do With All That Cash?" *Washington Post*, April 20, 2011, p. A7, available at http://www.washingtonpost.com/business/economy/chinas-3-trillion-dilemma-what-to-dowith-all-that-cash/2011/04/15/AFngE75D_story.html.

[45] CRS Report RL34314, *China's Holdings of U.S. Securities: Implications for the U.S. Economy*, by Wayne M. Morrison and Marc Labonte.

[46] For more information, see CRS Report RL33623, *Long-Term Measures of Fiscal Imbalance*, by D. Andrew Austin.

[47] President's Commission on Budget Concepts, *Report of the President's Commission on Budget Concepts*, October 1967.

[48] CRS Report RL30346, *Federal Credit Reform: Implementation of the Changed Budgetary Treatment of Direct Loans and Loan Guarantees*, by James M. Bickley.

[49] For details of federal budgetary control measures, see CRS Report R40610, *Federal Financial Management Reform: Past Initiatives and Future Prospects*, by Virginia A. McMurtry.

[50] U.S. Treasury, *Financial Report of the U.S. Government FY2010*, available at http://www.gao.gov/financial/fy2010financialreport.html.

[51] CBO, *Long-Term Budget Outlook*, June 2010, available at http://www.cbo.gov/doc.cfm?index=11579.

[52] CRS Report RL33657, *Running Deficits: Positives and Pitfalls*, by D. Andrew Austin.

[53] CBO, *Federal Debt and the Risk of a Fiscal Crisis*, issue brief, July 27, 2010, available at http://www.cbo.gov/doc.cfm?index=11659.

INDEX

G

H

I

P

R

S